BNP

OTHER EDITIONS IN THIS SERIES

George Garrett, guest editor, *Best New Poets 2005*

Eric Pankey, guest editor, *Best New Poets 2006*

Natasha Tretheway, guest editor, *Best New Poets 2007*

Mark Strand, guest editor, *Best New Poets 2008*

Kim Addonizio, guest editor, *Best New Poets 2009*

Claudia Emerson, guest editor, *Best New Poets 2010*

D.A. Powell, guest editor, *Best New Poets 2011*

Matthew Dickman, guest editor, *Best New Poets 2012*

Brenda Shaughnessy, guest editor, *Best New Poets 2013*

Dorianne Laux, guest editor, *Best New Poets 2014*

Tracy K. Smith, guest editor, *Best New Poets 2015*

Mary Szybist, guest editor, *Best New Poets 2016*

Natalie Diaz, guest editor, *Best New Poets 2017*

Kyle Dargan, guest editor, *Best New Poets 2018*

Cate Marvin, guest editor, *Best New Poets 2019*

Brian Teare, guest editor, *Best New Poets 2020*

Kaveh Akbar, guest editor, *Best New Poets 2021*

Paula Bohince, guest editor, *Best New Poets 2022*

BEST NEW POETS 2023

50 Poems from Emerging Writers

Guest Editor Anna Journey

Series Editor Jeb Livingood

This book is published in cooperation with *Meridian* (readmeridian.org) and the University of Virginia Press (upress.virginia.edu).

For additional information, visit us at
bestnewpoets.org
twitter.com/BestNewPoets
facebook.com/BestNewPoets

Cover design by 4 Eyes Design, 4eyesdesign.com

Text set in Adobe Garamond Pro and Droid Sans

Printed by Lightning Source

ISBN: 978-0-9975623-8-5
ISSN: 1554-7019

Contents

About *Best New Poets*

Welcome to *Best New Poets 2023*, our nineteenth annual anthology of fifty poems from emerging writers. At *Best New Poets* we define "emerging writer" narrowly: our anthology only features poets who have not yet published a book-length collection of their own poetry. Our goal is to provide special encouragement and recognition to poets just starting in their careers, the many writing programs they attend, and the magazines that publish their work.

From February to May of 2023, *Best New Poets* accepted nominations from writing programs and magazines in the United States and Canada. Each program and magazine could nominate two writers, and those poets could send a free submission to the anthology. For a small entry fee, writers could also submit poems as part of our open competition. Eligible poems were either published after January 1, 2022, or unpublished. Which means you are not only reading new poets in this book, but also some of their most recent work.

In all, we received just under 2,000 submissions for a total of nearly 3,700 poems. A pool of readers and the series editor ranked these submissions, sending a few hundred selections to this year's guest editor, Anna Journey, who chose the final fifty poems that appear here.

Guest Editor's Introduction

The year before my own work appeared in *Best New Poets 2006*, I was trying to figure out how to write a successful poem as an MFA student at VCU, in Richmond, Virginia. Mostly, though, I'd succeeded at getting fired from my summer job as a cashier in the outdoor lawn and garden section of Lowe's. The racket was that the hardware shop hired seasonal workers in early June, saying we'd keep the gig until school resumed in late August. Then management fired dozens of summer cashiers as soon as the Fourth of July passed. (The five weeks leading up to the Fourth were the store's big holiday shopping rush, but with geraniums and flat panel air filters instead of reindeer cut-outs and mistletoe.) I didn't feel much like a poet. I felt like a loser, walk-of-shaming past the not-fired employees as they lazed around the breakroom's lunch table, tossing me sympathetic looks, and out the automatic sliding doors onto Broad Street's humid shuffle. This is all to say that when my poem "Lucifer's Panties at Lowe's Garden Center"—which I wrote half out of revenge against my former employer and half out of genuine appreciation for the trippy names of hibiscus varieties—appeared in *BNP*, I felt less like a grad student mooching off her then-boyfriend for rent and more like a poet in the world. Because of this experience, I'm especially grateful for the opportunity to foreground fifty emerging writers for special recognition this year.

While the label "new" in *Best New Poets* is, for our purposes, straightforward (we meet these authors before they've published full-length collections), the designation "best," for any editor, remains subjective. I chose works for the anthology that evoke a distinct poetic voice, at times mature and at others dynamically evolving. The poems, an eclectic mix of styles and subject matter, have much in common: vivid imagery, clear occasions, inventive metaphors and turns of phrase, tonal authority, tension, and dramatic stakes that resonate. In these pages we encounter a variety of forms: sonnet, ghazal, sestina, villanelle, prose poem, haibun, erasure, abcedarian, multiple choice quiz, collage. We also find a range of genres: lyric, elegy, narrative, self-portrait, ekphrasis, ars poetica, ecopoem, lyric narrative, dramatic monologue, panegyric, fable. Throughout the course of the anthology, these poets tackle the Big Issues, those enduring beauties and brutalities of the human adventure: the death of a parent or sibling, lost loves, art that moves us, the desire to have/not have children, violence, war, the natural world, childhoods that haunt. They also interrogate a number of contemporary urgencies, such as the climate crisis and active shooters, as well as subjects that have for too long been stigmatized or unseen: sexual assault, suicide, gender dysphoria, abortion, addiction, caregiving for people with disabilities.

How about a preview? In Dāshaun Washington's "A Fairy Tale of Blackboyhood," a fabular prose poem about Blackness, masculinity, and notions of home, a twenty-one-year-old speaker receives a kiss from his father for the first time and transforms back into a child. "Sometimes—most times—I sleep with one eye open," the poet writes, "and hope to reunite with the strange magician who makes boys of men with forehead kisses." In Caitlin Roach's lyric narrative "Washington," set at low tide in a cove in the Pacific Northwest, the author meditates on the anxieties that thrum around a couple who take their young children to the beach (wildfires, pandemic, school shootings, a stranger's intravenous drug use, suicide in the news, a mother's cancer diagnosis). "Now we sift the sand // for needles," Roach writes with a mix of tenderness and apprehension, "tell our son we are helping him look / for crabs." In Juliana Chang's witty, anaphora-packed self-portrait "The Most Taiwanese Thing about Me," a yearbook misprint acts as an uncanny mirror for the speaker's sense of her own doubleness and cultural divisions:

> not my two passports
> or my two names.
> not the yearbook photo retake
> that made twins of me in second grade,
> Ting Wei and Juliana printed out
> side by side. not the time I made Kevin cry
> telling him Chang is a better last name
> than Zhang.

And in Julian Guy's complex reckoning with gender identity, "I Wake up and the House Is on Fire," a trans man meets his past self as a girl, both selves now united in a (literally and figuratively) burning house. Instead of a repudiation, we witness an abidingly protective enfolding:

> Heavy as a terracotta
>
> pot when I pick her up—rush us
> to the kitchen sink and spray water
> down our collars, our Good Lord
>
> Easter dresses. The ceiling
> collapsing. *Let's be bats*,
> she says, holding out the wings
>
> of her dress. *Yes*, I say,
> *Let's eat bugs*. I scoop her
> to my belly and we fly
>
> as heat needles our bodies
> down to stars, bright and
> dead already—Forgive me.
>
> I could not put her down.

I could not put down the poems in this anthology, its voices by turns grieving and wry, playful and anxious. I couldn't pick just one representative work from which to quote because this prismatic collection cleaves to no single form, genre, or aesthetic, no age group, demographic, or ideological framework. As Regan Green writes in her sly ars poetica, "On Shaving":

Only I know the secret patch
of blond on my kneecap
that always eludes the razor.
Landen says that in my poetry
I cut at a subject
from several different angles.
I should try this approach on my knee.

Poems have a way of doing that, don't they? Eluding the razor? Language as blade that would make clean work of the mystery. If only word-wrangling were that easy! Let's watch these poems refract and interact, these fine and "secret patches." Let's strike from different angles, and wait and see.

—Anna Journey

Anna Journey is the author of four poetry collections: *The Judas Ear* (2022), *The Atheist Wore Goat Silk* (2017), and *Vulgar Remedies* (2013), all from LSU Press, and *If Birds Gather Your Hair for Nesting* (University of Georgia Press, 2009), which was selected by Thomas Lux for the National Poetry Series. Her poems appear in *The New Yorker*, *The Kenyon Review*, *FIELD*, *The Southern Review*, and elsewhere. She's an associate professor of English at the University of Southern California.

Luciana Arbus-Scandiffio

Index of Me

alphabetically I am often the first
bastard of roll call bashful and beady-eyed
child of Linda and Marguerite I was born through
donor-insemination which makes me dangerous!
every day I am a daughter and every day I
field calls from unknown numbers on my phone *hello*
gainesville *hello hoosick falls* you could be anyone
holding me at arm's length there are half-siblings I've never met
I know Eli (ten months older) who lives in Seattle with his mothers I was
joking when I dangled his lucky blanket over the grill there was a
kite flying overhead we were sleeping in a tent
like wombats we bonded over the fountain of our faces drank too
much limeade couldn't find mars back home in
new jersey I was dim as a statue I spoke
only through signals wore a funny green hat was
private preferred mustard sat in the schoolyard like a
quilt sniffed flowers sniffed the social worker when she
ran out of games walked home on Wednesdays
struck through "father's name" with a pen
tried my best at badminton brought lunch in a paper bag
untied the borrowed sweater waved hi to principal
Vance at lunch they asked me *whichisyourrealmom*
whosthedad I am eight but I will take an
X-ACTO knife to your face you'd never see me coming
you'd only see a flurry of hands I am a
zoo I am a zoo and I will make a mess of you

—Nominated by *Washington Square Review*

Alicia Rebecca Myers

G Day

Today is G Day, my son says to me
the morning after another school shooting
he doesn't yet know about. The alphabet countdown
has begun to mark the passage of time between
now and the final class when second graders stream
out the guarded door and into summer. *We're learning*
about grapes, he says, and as I unknot his hair,
hands shaking, I picture the kids in a criss-cross
circle, eyes closed, each biting excitedly into
a succulent spherical berry before giving language
to the pop: *Sweet and tart* or *like jelly.* And there
will certainly be a child who thinks but maybe doesn't
say, *the shape of a bullet*, the way his teacher will keep
her terror private, the way I hear in my head, *G is for gun*.

Shirley Stephenson

Calibrate

It's done annually, like the observance
of a religious holiday or paying taxes,

this redetermination of rightness. We cross-
check and re-set the sphygmomanometer

and centrifuge so that we can gauge
and dose and spin the blood with accuracy.

At the end-of-shift, we stack the collection
tubes like shotgun shells in the lockbox

outside the door, where each night
an arsenal of ruby and gold awaits

its courier. From the Arabic *qalib*, a mold
for making ammunition, comes *caliber*:

the interior diameter of the barrel.
In June, the clinic's security cameras caught

a crowd pulling a couple out of their car.
The man was killed as he knelt

over the woman. The bullets spun
and spun their life into its separate

components. The bullets splintered,
tore, and lodged. There's no way to say

what all the bullets can do to a person.
Mourners and politicians gathered

at the site for days until city workers
plowed away the flowers and doused

the stain with bleach. Still, we stepped
around it. Friends of the dead woman

described her as a good mother,
a good soul. *Calibre*, from the late

fifthteenth-century French: a quality of character.
Against what instrument can we

measure this? Are my ventricles full
enough? Do I have the heart?

Ending with *-ate* signifies an action
taken, as in *separate*, or a state of being,

as in *desperate.* The detectives who came
to review the clinic's footage were sorry

to interrupt patient care. The motive
remained unclear but they'd found

the 9mm shells and forensic analysis,
they assured us, is an exact science.

No one, said the cop, should adjust
to this. It goes against all standards.

Samyak Shertok

Love in a Time of Revolution

Between 1996 and 2006, an internal conflict between the Government of Nepal and the Communist Party of Nepal (Maoist) left at least 13,000 people dead and 1,300 missing, and an estimated 200,000 displaced.

It happened.

/

I write to you from across the Mikli-Phoom that cannot break.

/

We met once in three months. We met
for two minutes. We never met
in rain. We met
only during the party programs. We met
with a comrade watching us. We met
when the moonbugs were drunk on heat. Every time we met,
we exchanged bullets. We never met.
I only knew her from the letters.

/

He was five years younger. I worked with him
organizing programs in the adjoining VDC's. He
addressed me as didi and would try to come closer. He
wrote asking if he could visit me. He asked me what my
perspective towards him was. *Positive* I wrote him back.
He proposed to me to sit and talk. *Barberry thorns* I said.

No age in love he said. *The proletarian hand does not count silver*… Next day we put in an application to the party.

/

No child ~~marriage~~
No arranged ~~marriage~~
No forced ~~marriage~~
No ~~dowry~~
No ~~bride~~ price
No ~~polygamy~~
No ~~premarital sex~~
Love ~~marriage~~
Janabādi ~~marriage~~
No ~~caste~~
No ~~class~~

/

… even after getting married I always lived with my friends. I felt uneasy about staying with him in front of other comrades. Once the meeting of our party committee was going to be held in his village. His family had already made an arrangement. He came with a sleeping bag and sat beside me…

/

Bury the bayonet: open the marigold.

/

In the seventh year, I became double-bodied. I was
reassigned to the cultural group. While I was dancing the Red
Dance, the child of the revolution danced himself out.

/

Bride of the Revolution. Blindfolded Hornets. Crossfire-caught Love.
We entered the rhododendron forest to make revolution—not love.

"Because they cannot forget, the stars burn in their own light." The enemy
slaughtered Operation Golden Jackal from within. With love, we fought love.

The bullhorn spluttered: *We've surrounded you from all four directions.* The sky
broke pink with the handwritten leaflets, signed: *Touch-Me-Nuts, Love.*

Then arrived the list: Hero Honda, wedding bed, 24-karat bracelet,
milk buffalo… I loaded the cartridge. Without moving a finger, I bought love.

They made our fathers eat *Kantipur*, peed on the dirt shrouding our sisters' naked hair.
Yet in the pit, even the Kauravas—*In the name of Krishna, please shoot us!*—sought love.

After the vermillion oath, I didn't see him for two years. When our platoons
finally crossed paths, I saw his eyes were emptied—not even the sickle-wrought love?

To know it said the sadhu *you must become it.* The pressure cooker
in his Onepolar backpack, the boy bloomed into what could not be taught: love

for samsara bereft of himself. Rainless monsoon. Our lips split like tinder.
A firefly flashed: *Enemy in the branches!* We fired at the moon: our bloodshot love.

Ammo-less. No reinforcements. After six days and seven nights of fighting
on only Thin Arrowroot biscuits, we forgot the enemy, forgot love.

Read my diary to my daughter, then burn it. Feed the yellowjackets my blood
from your barbwired palm. Jackal me. Vulture me. But let my love not rot, Love.

Eight battles, shrapnelled eye, one kill, three stars: still the moonbugs haunt
my moon. What river—your name?—could cool this Kalash-throat, Love?

/

A betel nut knocked on the door. *Mangal has risen* said Ama. *Mangal will not rise again* said Ama. The school was pamphlet-locked, and if you stayed home unwed, they would come for you. Without seeing the groom, I bit the nut.

Pablo Piñero Stillmann

Present

My mother brings home a soccer ball: sixteen red panels
& their white twins. It hangs from a string net,
also red, that my mother helps me cut with her ruby scissors.
There isn't enough space in the apartment to play,
so I carry the ball around like a pet rabbit. The ball
watches TV with me. During the spaghetti Bolognese
dinner, the ball takes what was my father's chair
& can't see a thing. When I go to bed, the ball replaces
my stuffed ladybug. The following morning I bring the ball
to school so all can play with it. But as we flood out
to recess, I remember everyone always plays with Jorge's
black-and-white Adidas. Everyone loves Jorge. We're not
close to adolescence & yet some girls come to school
wearing their mothers' cherry or apple nail polish
in hopes he will notice them. I take the ball with me
on a tour of the grounds: to the cafeteria, the library,
the parking lot, all the way to the high school gym, &
to the middle school building where my sister's getting an A.
The ball & I sit nowhere in sight. I ask it how my mother's
able to do all: work, take care of us, drive for hours under
the dirty sun—even date sometimes. I ask the ball if my father
misses me & if I'll fail. It doesn't know. How could it?
Then I ask what happened to its family. The ball says
they were killed by a rebel army that left most
of its faraway country splattered in blood. "That's why
I'm half red," says the ball. "I'm tainted with the suffering
of those before me." First thing back home that afternoon,

I hide the ball in my closet & try to forget about it. Years
later, when we move, one of the movers steals it, & that
night, drunk as a goddamn coral snake, the mover wakes
his son to present the gift. It's the only time he'll tell the boy
he loves him. I hope the boy comes to realize his father is a thief.

—Nominated by *Gettysburg Review*

Ira Goga

Faggots

All day in my head I say the name for them.
I kneel and take   thick as pipe   the bundle
of sticks.   In the sugarhouse   I feed
the furnace.   I tend the heat, deep kiss
of woodsmoke up my neck.   Concentrating
the sap over hours.   Paring the water,   pooling the sugar,
reducing its form   to make it sweeter.   I blow
on the spoon   before I swallow and still burn   my tongue.
          When I was a dyke,
men disgusted me,   their roughness. The hemlock logs,
sawed and split,   stacked into cords. What pleasure
there was in being tied   to certainty, lashed
to an identity,   to be legible   to those whom I desire.
Sticky at the finish,   dripping in strands,
the syrup golden and delicate.
          At the boiler's core,
like a season I'm distant from,   a lightness—the coals
bright as peaches.

—Nominated by *DIALOGIST*

Dennison Ty Schultz

Today I'm Not Thinking about Gender So

let's say it's August ! let's say I'm drinking sun rays from a faucet ! let's say the sun

loops around to slather clay on my forehead & nipples ! let's say the air is a smoothie

of mango & dandelion yolk ! let's say my longing was designed by fire ants ! wait let's say

it's July July bites the lip of August it's almost August July snuggled deep in its burrow ! let's say the stones

peeling through mulch are honed by heat ! let's say the wasp nests & their chorusmouths

ringaling with morning ! let's say I know home best when buried in it ! let's say the figs dingdinging vibrato

sappy on their branches ! let's say there's clay sweatthick on my neck clay all over brimming my neck orange

streaking down my back ! let's say I nibble itty bitty honeydews off rosebushes

as a treat ! let's say I know home best when kept from it ! let's say popsicles are plummyyummy

glorious suited in their syrup bikinis ! let's say my silly suction cup brain ! let's say the walkway in flame like a lip

bitten with bird's eyes ! let's say oh no encyclopedias spilled & wrinkling like sidewalk worms ! let's say hummingbirds

whoopsydaisy on nectar until their necks dizzy ! let's say wiggling toes little toesies leaving

shells in the wet asphalt ! let's say this body is a point of conjecture ! let's say the sun's voice ripples choppedgrassy

& gravelly with cantaloupes ! & the sun says here is the light (!) don't you want to look at me !

Anthony Borruso

Murphy's Law

Thirty rabies shots, my uncle got
when, after cornering a rat for fun,
and drunk, it lept and bit his bare chest.

Play stupid games, win stupid prizes, they
say—*what can happen, will*—Which is what
my dad was thinking when he passed the pub

so aptly named on the day they sawed
through my skull. This is the perversity
of the universe. You go outside

to catch your breath and butcher's knives wink
in every window. Miles's trumpet intones
So What while atom bombs dream of flouting

their dormancy. The night before surgery,
I lay on the plush hotel bed, staring
at a room service form. When I was

little, I was obsessed with opulence.
I wanted filet mignon, lobster
delivered to my imagined penthouse

as I watched cartoons: a toddler bobbing
along the steel girders of a nascent
skyscraper, pianos crashing down, turning teeth

into sonatas. Sometimes you have
to confront the world's malice like a mouse
who's been burned too many times by spring-

loaded-cheese. I remember assuming
the hospital's food would be suspect.
Juice with plastic peel-off top, overly-

salted soup, but, I thought: that's only
if they don't slice into my temporal
lobe. If they don't accidentally

give me a lobotomy, or cut my
head clean off. I'll be lucky to gag
on pot pie while mom scrolls WebMD.

—Nominated by *Aquifer: The Florida Review Online*

Alice White

Multiple Choice

Select all that apply.

I had been at
a) my friend's wedding
b) a ritual sacrifice
c) a congress of ghosts

It was
a) the first time I met my friend's fiancé
b) the last time I saw my friend

I was wearing
a) my big sister's yellow silk dress
b) heels that cut into my heels
c) an amulet made of amethyst

At the reception afterward I was
a) tipsy
b) drunk
c) roofied

I remember
a) spilling red wine on a white tablecloth
b) burning my hands with candle wax
c) him helping me

I brought him home with me because
a) he was alone
b) I was alone
c) we are all alone

We
a) had sex
b) did not have sex

I
a) consented
b) did not consent

In the morning I
a) looked for clues and found none
b) drove him home, thirty minutes away, in silence
c) tried to obtain a morning-after pill
d) was covered in volcanic ash, the expression on my face
perfectly preserved

I remember
a) flashes of him on top of me
b) flashes of pushing him away

I don't remember
a) his name
b) the way home
c) convincing my roommate I was okay

I was
a) a slut
b) a victim

c) a twenty-something
d) a human being

It was
a) my fault
b) his fault
c) no one's fault
d) everyone's fault

I should have
a) not worn that dress
b) not had that beer
c) not brought him home
d) left with a ghost

After this, I did not have sex for
a) five years
b) six years

After this, he had sex
a) the next night
b) the next week
c) as soon as he had the chance

He
a) remembers me
b) does not remember me

He could have been
a) a predator
b) a nice guy who was just also drunk
c) the father of my child

If I had gotten pregnant, I would have
a) had an abortion
b) had a baby
c) sprouted wings and flown through a hole in the sky

If I had gotten pregnant, he would have
a) cared
b) not cared
c) never known

When asked how many people I've slept with, I
a) include him
b) do not include him
c) do the same thing for the other time this happened

Lina Herman

Before We Rushed Our Daughter to the Hospital

It's 3:10 on Wednesday this past Wednesday three days ago
I'd skipped the *Next Steps* and *Check-Out*
sections of my team's quarterly planning meeting
to get Louisa to Bayview Park early for after school surf camp
she likes to pull her wetsuit on before they head down to Cole Point
I get home in time to whip heavy cream we are going low fat high carb
I mean high fat low carb I hear Isabel's world history teacher on speaker
begging the kids to turn in something anything by Friday
when he lets her class out she comes to the kitchen she zips and unzips
her brown velour sweatshirt with daisies embroidered on the pockets
she asks me what I'm doing now and I tell her about my quick snack
before my 3:30 debrief call I eat the cream with blueberries and pecans
out back under our avocado tree I like the way the sun lands soft
for my few extra minutes I choose between *The New York Times Daily*
and my urban paranormal fantasy audiobook I can't remember which I pick
probably the shapeshifter novel that's what I like when work is piled on
I bring my bowl and spoon and mason jar still half-filled with sparkling water
back to the kitchen Jacob has come home early wearing his navy tie
he picks at the leftover cheese from my ranch salad I had wanted
to at least wash the whisk before my call I hate it when people in this house
leave the whisk in the sink it seems so delicate like it will get crushed
under dirty dishes though it never has but it's also nice
to lean against the counter and chat about what was it bike riding
at the waterfront maybe or defrosting salmon for dinner
I thought you were in the bathroom he says and I wonder out loud
why heavy cream tastes so much better in its whipped form
when Isabel comes in shaking crying arms crossed

her hair in a low ponytail strands hanging loose
gripping two empty amber prescription bottles
hair falling out of her ponytail all those strands
and tells us she swallowed all the pills

Jasmine Khaliq

Ghazal for My Father

At birth they named him Ashar, *one who has wisdom,* his head
Was so big. *Ashar,* a cupped hand, holding up his newborn head.

I know little of his life then. Orange sweets, wet Augusts, movie theatres.
Eldest son, brightest student, hardest worker. Taller than all his brothers by a head.

Born in Punjab—province where, twenty-three hundred years earlier,
Bucephalus met his end. *A massive creature with a massive head—*

Whatever you imagine will not be him. Archaic torso, Ashar, young and not yet
Graying, watching football, my father, American. Bending sunglasses to fit his head.

My mother, when I am stubborn, says, *You really are his daughter. You know, you are*
Just like him. Sometimes, I like this. Or I remind her I inherited her peanut head,

Her anxiety, her mother's mouth, her mother's wrists. Or I might blame being a Taurus,
Reading books about dark, stubborn horses. *Bucephalus* meaning *ox-head.*

In Hayward, at a baby shower, aunties I'd never met said, *you're lucky*
You don't have your father's nose, so prominent on his head—

In fact, they said, I look like women from the region Alexander the Great's men conquered
And settled, how blessed. I was fourteen. Flattered. Blood rushing to the head.

It's not impossible. Untraceable lines, name changes, colonization.
I too can impose anything on it. Once I spoke of a veil that would cover my head

When I got married—my great-great-grandmother's, passed
Daughter to daughter, Catholic, long, lace-trimmed. No veil exists. In my head

I wear it, talking with my grandmother in heaven. Walking, I feel it drag
Against every green hedge. Bridal, I meet Bucephalus. Touch his ancient head.

Tell me about Pakistan, I say, I've never been. And whatever I imagine incorrect.
Pakistan, he says, *haven't heard of it.* Chews on me like a lettuce head.

Or, a man's—Bucephalus, we hear, descended from flesh-eating mares. Me,
No essence, no frame. History of which I can't make tail nor head;

No veil. Last summer, my father broke his nose falling face-first from a scooter,
Smoothed its bump into an easy Appalachian slope, changed his whole head.

Free nose job, he joked, but I cried over it. The profile he'd had all his life, all mine,
Made myth. It doesn't matter, but it did. I'm caught off-guard when he turns his head.

He is wise, to embrace it. It's just—I know so little of his life then.
What did he dream of? Giant horses? A daughter with a narrow head?

In California, in a little pot, my father plants the national flower of Pakistan. Common
Jasmine, poet's jasmine, white jasmine, true jasmine: all the same flower to crown my head.

Annie P. Quigley

Portrait with My Two Grandmothers

The sun comes up and coats
our street in melted butter,
sickle moon still out, a shard of hard candy
in the mouth. Gram writes me a message
in the ice on the windshield, it says
Oh the world is good,
there is still butter and the knuckle meat
of lobsters, there is still ginger,
and I wish she were sitting in my living room right now,
bickering, glasses on a chain
around her neck, perm and thermos
of ginger ale. My other grandmother
has jet-black hair and is always
young. The only time they were in the same place
on this earth in their brief
and briefer lifetimes
was a green hill on the hottest day
of summer in 1984, ankles
crossed, in peach. I have the photos
and their blood in me, thrumming,
and every story, divided:
the one that is true
and the one my sister and I have heard.
When I hear it from my aunts,
I only half believe it. They say she
[redacted]. They say she [blank].

The stories last
all night. My sister wonders
if she burned the house down
on purpose but I can't think
of that, the cigarette at the end
of her long fingers,
how burned they would be, the way
a trained eye could tell, crouching,
what started it all
but couldn't see
the night in France her husband looked out
and saw her in the garden,
dancing. My aunts say she
was never the same.
I was never human
at the same time she was human
but I wear her ring
on my finger,
and sometimes
the rivulet vein in that finger
pulses in Morse code,
or it could, and if she left me
a message I imagine it would say careful.
Or: Is there such a thing
as being too alive?

Nick Martino

Polaroid: Prison Visit

November 22, 1989

Paper plates table scraps Paper documents
the case against my father
is his leaning away
the moment his love fell off?
show it to me— their divorce
dead pines behind
flock of pigeons mid-air the shadow of a red-tailed
hawk my mother gripping an unlit match between her teeth
the fire I feed
nicotine gum Blue book of matches
my mother's right hand
gazes at the ground save them.

Paper plates litter the picnic table, scraps from the day's visitation. Paper documents from the case against my father. My mother squinting through the winter sun, collar turned to the wind, her hand on his back, his leaning away—is there a different kind of evidence here? Can I find the moment his love fell off? I'm looking for the image to show it to me—the second, fossilized, their divorce took root from a crystal seed from which our brittle house would grow. As if dead pines behind my parents mean anything. As if the flock of pigeons frozen mid-air invents the shadow of a red-tailed hawk. Is it a fool's errand: my mother gripping an unlit match between her teeth, me dreaming of the fire taking shape in her mind? I imagine the fire. I feed it with detail like kindling—nicotine gum, two cans of Pepsi. Blue book of matches, three chapters missing. Hemmed red in the cold, my mother's right hand is pointing to an elsewhere beyond the frame. My father gazes at the ground. I need it to be me who saves them.

Caitlin Roach

Washington

We thought it was a dead thing—the colorless flesh
stems' pendants sagging toward the underworld

from which they fed, a parasite feeding
on another parasite—but it wasn't. Everywhere

moss slick as fish on rocks, on logs, bracken
fern sprawling like sea stars sucking

the barnacled slabs we scramble at low tide.
Nearby, my son's voice like an echo

threads through the shore pines to the tidepools
where he watches the sugar wrack's

smooth blades billowing silk-like
in the quiet water. The first time

I bring my sons to this sea, a man
my age sat alone on the shore

shooting up. He shielded the needle
with his coat, a gesture of courtesy

or shame I nevertheless respected.
My son searched for sea glass and the man

slipped deep into his sweet dream as the cove
readied to glow and the anemones opened like sores

dumbed to the threat of my son's plunging
finger. He lay in the cold, flush with the heat of it

rushing through him, but I did not
yet have the memory of the Chinook

boring through their natal river's rapids
by the granary, their huge bodies slapping

the rocks like thick paddles, to conjure. I lie
and say I see the plankton giving off their cold light

at the other end of the beach
to let the dreamer dream in quiet, then

a lesson on luciferin and
bioluminescence. Now we sift the sand

for needles, tell our son we are helping him look
for crabs. In our first half year here, time pitches

impossibly. The baby stumbles
into his first steps, the older boy begins dreaming

in daylight away from us, finds himself
in a stranger's arms when he slips and hits

his head. I am the only one
to cry. There is the virus that levels us

with the same spell that lands my mother
in hospital, her memory wiped like a bright spot

burned into nothing, her stare on the screen
so blank it bore chills, the mind a light

year away, and the cancer diagnosis validating
illogical fear, and the surgery that came after that

black November night when a woman
lurched in front of the train—the one

the baby signals he hears each morning,
his hand to his ear, grunting—barreling

through the dark we drove through
with our sons looking at Christmas lights

blooming like wet orbs in the rain. I read
days later she was a mother

and stop there. Before this there is rain
and rain and rain. You couldn't believe

what the rhododendrons do around here.
There is the blue heron we see slide

on the lake, on the lawn, in the sky,
the hollyhocks flagging their big bells

all down the sidewalk, that hot August
and blackberries invasive as lantern-

flies. There are the fires that turn the sun
a pale pink orb over the bay, the smoke

swallowing even that sun, shutting everyone in
for days from the toxic haze we'd learn

was clutching the lungs of our sons.
There are the too-bright mornings

I bring the baby outside in the yard while I wait
for the older boy to wake, flocks of black

birds unspooling like ribbon above us.
There is the story that breaks the week

of our son's third birthday of fifty-three migrants
who suffocated to death in a semi in Texas,

the five on the muted screen newly recognizable
to him as he shouts *cinco!* and is proud

of this, his other language, borne to him
by his father who migrated north

as a child, too—and still we must put on
a good face. There is the first bee sting

and the heat waves and the hundred-acre woods
we walk in nearly naked to escape them, then

the threat of an active shooter at the high school
thirty yards from our son's preschool. Then

months of violent dreaming. Eventually
the salmon run ends. The dark

season siphons everything out
from the light one and there's nothing we can do

about any of it. In different weeks
our firstborn asks *what is die, what is kill,*

what is spirit, says the saddest part of his day
is seeing the injured buck limp

across the mud hill out back. Says *Mama*
do you know what bad dream I had?

We were walking by a steam train
and it extincted you and I was calling for you

and you didn't call back. I couldn't
script it. He learns of the world

this way, holding the pain of others
in his small body, the flush

of proxy anger he feels when I am angry
with his father, translates the baby's

pre-verbal music into material
we can hold onto. Every time he is right,

knows his exact need. *Think this*
he says seriously in our playful argument

about whom loves the other more
we both love each other even

more. Kelp strips stick to the baby's
cold thigh and even in this cruel dark

the cove glows, pulsing white-bright. *Okay*
I reply. *Yes. You are right* and let the lie steep

like plankton in their heatless light.

Christine Byrne

Cups

Grog into clay on a canvas table—I'm wedging—
while Irene drags a space heater to the center of the room—
using a clementine peel—as an ashtray—
in the old barn studio—I've been watching things harden—
your bike stopped short—on the pine road—
stomach against the handlebars—had to get your spleen out—
I liked—that something was missing in you—things were constantly—
getting lost in me—I knead—
until we gutter—the cold water—dragging stock pots through the snow—
Irene fingers her scalp for bald spots—saying it's stress—that there are ways—
the body talks—
your father—drank my perfume—
kissed each of my shoulders, slowly—kneeling on the carpet—
you, on the green recliner—
I was watching tides in places where there were none—
etching the sides of cups—I open—
my hands—with their flaking bits—
if I could vitrify—if I could read grief—
like telling by a highway—how bad a winter gets someplace—
scooping droppings up—from the field mice—capping wax resist—
scraping slabs off the kick wheel—thawing my hands in lukewarm water—
there were moments I thought—watching you split wood out the kitchen window—
slamming in a wedge—resting the sledgehammer soft thump in the grass—
turning to look at me—
that this—would be all my life—pools of stagnant water—
making you a cup—that you'll weigh up & down—
peek inside of, saying—this—is a good one—

Maria Esquinca

Death Fragments: On Loving My Mother

Every day seems like the beginning of another death.

-

HEADLINE: COVID-19 HAS REACHED THE SOUTH POLE

-

The California sun ombres the Fresno sky into a sunset. It's so beautiful I almost forget the fires smothering the heavens.

-

HEADLINE: MAN MURDERED OWN BROTHER, FRESNO COUNTY SHERIFF'S OFFICE SAYS

-

What drives a man to kill a part of himself?

-

The first sense we develop is sound. Inside our mother's womb all we can do is listen.

-

It snowed in El Paso in October. Even the desert is not itself.

-

HEADLINE: 'IT LOOKS LIKE DOOMSDAY': CALIFORNIA RESIDENTS REACT TO ORANGE SKY

-

My brother, finally fed up with my mother, tells me he's going to move out of her house. She took his car and crashed it, left it to rot blaze in an empty field like a fist in flames.

-

I wonder if my neighbor heard me crying in my office.

-

HEADLINE: WHISTLEBLOWER SAYS EL PASO AMBULANCES PICKING UP COVID-19 PATIENTS FROM JUÁREZ
Comment: *why are those coming from cd. juarez not going to hospitals in cd. Juarez?*

-

I'm trying to find the language for betrayal.

-

I want to change the parts of me that are most like my mother, which is almost all of me.

-

My aunt sends me a slow-mo video of my cousin jumping on a snow-covered trampoline. Snow cascades around her body like confetti. Suspended joy.

-

YOUTUBE VIDEO: WHY DON'T MY RELATIONSHIPS WORK? ADULT CHILDREN OF ALCOHOLICS

aStoneMirror: 4 weeks ago
Will we ever heal?

-

El Paso mayor, Dee Margo, says Hispanics are not like regular people. They die at higher rates.

-

There's a church forest in Ethiopia. In order to be considered a church it has to be surrounded by a forest. To be close to the trees is to be close to God. Because of over-grazing the forests are getting destroyed, so farmers built a wall around the forest to protect it. How strange, that a wall can turn itself inward.

-

Some walls can do the opposite of divide and be divine.

-

PSYCHOLOGY VIDEO: "EMOTIONS ARE MEANT TO PROTECT US"

-

I imagine myself hanging from the rail of my closet like the tresses of my dresses. A comatose jellyfish.

-

HEADLINE: AGENTS SAVE MAN STUCK HANGING OVER OCEAN ON BORDER WALL

-

I know God exists when I stand next to a sequoia tree at Yosemite. 275 feet tall. Its trunk wider than my two arms spread apart around its trunk.

-

In El Paso they begin to hire "morgue attendants." $27 an hour. The posting closes within days because so many people apply.

-

To love my alcoholic mother is a lesson in not being able to protect those I love.

-

The sun will die one day. It dims, then explodes. Will become a blackhole. Out of all the science lessons I wasn't taught the one about how the suns are stars, or the stars are suns. How they have a lifespan. Just like us.

-

HEADLINE: STOCKHOLM POLICE HAVE ARRESTED A WOMAN SUSPECTED OF KEEPING HER 41-YEAR-OLD SON CONFINED TO THEIR FLAT FOR ALMOST THREE DECADES

-

My dad tells me that the hospitals in Juárez are so full they can't take in new patients. People are dying in their homes.

-

Fall looks pretty in Fresno. The treetops smear the drive with colors: magenta, saffron, amethyst, scarlet, cerise, some so bright they look like Moses's burning bush.

-

Even then, in her womb, I must've loved my mother. Before I knew what love was and all I had were bits of her syllables handed to me through flesh and belly.

-

HEADLINE: TRUMP PARDONS INCLUDE TWO BORDER PATROL AGENTS WHO SHOT UNARMED MIGRANT WOMAN

-

Eventually all of space will die too. They call it entropy. We're not so different from the cosmos, you and I.

Tina Blade

Vine Maple

I remember when Mom asked me just before she died,
Tina, was I a good mother? This small-town girl
who loved dancing and mink—asked me as if she didn't know.
The vine maple at the window leaned in and touched the glass.

I was thinking. I was thinking *You were not a good mother.*
I didn't know she was brave to ask. I didn't know she'd missed me.
The vine maple at the window leaned in, its thin branches
lifted, graceful as the arms of a girl.

I refused to think she was brave. I didn't know I'd miss her.
I hated what I remembered: her brandy, her dancing, the smell of her cigarettes,
the branches reaching—for her or for me? Whose arms? Which girl?
I knew the dry sound in the afternoon of the liquor cabinet opening.

I hated her drinking, her dancing, her cigarettes. I loved
the smell of her Joy perfume. How might she be different if she didn't drink?
I listened for the click of the liquor cabinet opening.
I prayed for the day that door would stay shut.

How would I be different if she didn't drink?
Was I a good mother? she asked at the very last minute,
the cabinet door forever opening and closing.
This small-town girl asking me, as if I of all people would know.

—Nominated by *Apple Valley Review*

Julian Guy

I Wake Up and the House Is on Fire

I'm a woman again. The surgery
undone—the scars folded back
into skin. Pillowy breasts hang

freckled, fat. I am my mother's
daughter. My father's trophy.
The dresses I gave away float back

down the hall like floral ghosts,
smoke pluming in from the vents.
In the bathroom mirror, a soft face,

cheeks peach fuzzy and plump, not
pockmarked by second puberty.
My high school lipstick, *Red*

Lizard, on the counter. A long O
of my mouth, and I put myself
together. My mustache gone,

the motions of girlhood returning.
The floor hot under the hearts
of my feet. I leave myself

and there I am, five years old
on the couch and the whole
house is burning. Heavy as a terracotta

pot when I pick her up—rush us
to the kitchen sink and spray water
down our collars, our Good Lord

Easter dresses. The ceiling
collapsing. *Let's be bats*,
she says, holding out the wings

of her dress. *Yes*, I say,
let's eat bugs. I scoop her
to my belly and we fly

as heat needles our bodies
down to stars, bright and
dead already—Forgive me.

I could not put her down.
Even past the house that stood
or did not in the night

behind us. I could not be sure
we were still alive,
even when the stars melted

into a sky so lavender I cried
real tears—and the horizon did not
close, and our dresses fell away

and so did my feet, they fell,
too, and the road kept running
on without us and my arms

grasped air and our bodies
changed—I swear they did,
cause we were flying

over the city of my life
and I loved her. I did not
let her go.

Anthony Thomas Lombardi

speed trap town

like the sky i've been lingering, too quiet
for invocation. there's nothing here
that can't be left behind—the peonies blushing
only a week before they wilt, the spirits & smolder
that came home in my curls. *a ship tethered to its dock*
cannot wreck, the old-timer once crooned
at a daytime meeting, spreading his arms
as if to mean, *all of this*.
that night, i snuck a bottle up the bleachers
& forgot my name, cried at the wrong
kitchen table, learned to wrap a bandage
with one hand. i welcomed the wisteria's war
on the brand new condos, the thrushes
building their nest above walkways
sheltering a parade of soft targets. some of you
will be dead next year. my big brother learned young
how small a handful it takes.
i just turned older than him.
years ago under a hunter's moon
i stayed awake just to watch him
glow, campfire & perfume in his wild hair.
he smelled a little like a train, darkened skin
of a summer shade. i don't remember this, i was told
—go home, kick the clutch & drive slow
as a volcano, far enough to find Heaven
burns more gravel than grief.

you can't wash a floor with a bucket of dirty water
an empty chair murmurs between days counted
& nights renounced. *but it's put out enough fires*
i never replied. in New York, the MTA created a job
cleaning up train tracks after suicides.
no one lasts more than a month or two
i'm told. i pray the peonies receive clemency
past sunset, a landslide not pyrrhic but pearled.
i pray the wisteria kisses every inch of baked brick
in the projects i was raised, warm & caressed
as a coffin's handles. i pray a trampled nest of wasps
alight on nectar, sailing past swooping hands
all of this. all of this before you got here.

Emily Alexander

Who I Am

By evening I'm feeling bad
about my body again,
convinced the chokecherry trees are mocking me
for my weird knees and looking up
teleology six times
before knowing what it means.

Annoyed with C all weekend for no good reason.
Sometimes I can't tell what's real between us
and what I've invented
or reconstructed via complex negotiations
with the flimsy framework of memory.

Archery practice ages ago,
his head, my shoulder.
All my arrows missed the target
and shooting the fake deer in the echoey gymnasium
still kind of drunk for three elective credits
was a bad metaphor for our indecipherable relationship
but still pretty funny.

Kind of like when I served bad lasagna
at the Italian joint across from the fountain downtown
and it didn't mean anything.
I deposited my little pittance
every other Friday in exchange for humming along
to Mambo Italiano four times a night

all ha ha ha uncorking bottles
of mediocre pinot for corny tasteless patrons
in matching polo shirts.

With Janey in Rome
that summer we were beautiful and walking everywhere.
We ate pasta and played cards in the club.
I was in love with a man
who appears antlike to me now
like all along I'd been looking at him through a telescope
while he stood tinily beside me,
acting so zoomed in.
Janey cut my hair with children's scissors.
I bought a thong at the grocery store,
cheap black lace. We each had our own irretrievable feelings
crossing the laughable traffic together.

Does humor deflect sincerity
or reinforce it? Little pylons for holding
a long dark train.

It matters to me, being seen,
said Halle one night in a bar on Nineteenth. And yet
I resent the imprecision of these gazes.
She gestured then, and I saw
that we were surrounded
or spotlit in a way. How vain
and unrelenting this desire is.
To be taken in.

It used to be with C I thought: this person
throws me into focus.
Now we laugh at each other's jokes.

Maybe it's that I don't think it's fun anymore
to feel so horrible and sit around until night,
resigned to lackluster Tuesdays
in the cheap snowglobes of our lives—
the unvarying plastic mountain range
of some interminable winter.
Maybe we outgrew the misery
of that particular hiccup of youth,
and all those nights when what was inscrutable in me
did not necessarily disappear
but was held
or mirrored or made graspable by what
was inscrutable in him
were really just two people in the dark,
but I miss being near him unblurred.

The other night I went out with the guy opening
New York's first Jimmy John's sandwich shop.
Having just come from work
I wore clogs and ketchup on my shirt
and picked at the stain while he told me
about zoning laws and a permit-based complication
that would likely require litigation,
delaying what was meant to be
a freaky fast grand opening.
I was sipping gold liquid
that tasted like honey and all the lights of the city
from a rooftop on a half-warm night
where I'm always wanting to be and wanting to leave.
I was thinking about the word audacity,
how I always feel like
here are people

and here is me,
and I'm some sort of comically limping cartoon
falling off sudden cliffs
into the far below briar patch of afternoon.
I wonder if that's true
or just a shape I've invented and now
given name to.
It's like I've been shot
raftless down a difficult river,
but really it's morning.
I'm drinking coffee in New York City.

Then there was the guy with the sun and moon tattoo
who fingered me while I slept.
They're both smiling, he told me, because
it's important in life to stay positive.
Elbows, ankles, inner thighs.
How it was not as big a deal as I thought it would be,
just pretending to like it and waiting for him to leave.

I feel like a Mario kart full throttling into the wall.
Do you feel this way or are you normal?
This is a popular internet joke
but I'd really like to know
which of my idiosyncrasies are acceptable
and which I should keep,
as they say, on the down low.

I texted C and he took a day to reply.
Maybe I was trying to reach the version of him from the past.
Maybe I was trying to reach the version of me from the past.
Maybe I was trying to be a specific person,

not a nakedness saying yes, a clattering
of practiced obscenities.

Laughing with Dylan in the empty restaurant,
wineglass wobbling almost imperceptibly now,
now still, I said watching you is how I imagine it is watching me.
How it is watching me is impossible
to know with any certainty.
There are emails and Shrek the Musical and cheese boards.
There are four cups of coffee maddening my heartbeat.
There are many kinds of people with varying blueprints of desire.
I forget what I liked about poetry.

Then I found myself walking in Brooklyn.
It was August and evening and the tops of the buildings
were cut off by sunlight.
I thought maybe I was a person losing,
but someone was giving someone a cigarette
and there were several ceramic dog statues gazing out from the stoop,
and I was there among them
losing and giving and gazing and walking and walking.

Aurora Shimshak

Pill Abortion

How intimate
we become with light
when emptied. My blinds ebbing

apricot sun, replay
of our feral hips, me
in a koi fish sundress,

our pretending
to be homesteaders
in my grandparents' vacant house.

At the clinic, the nurse
asked if I feared losing my job,
but I had only imagined

a chain-link
fence, a flat town,
a lack of exits.

My lover came over and paced
while I bled, as I studied
my star births in toilet water—

lilliputian nebulae of the not-mom,
not today, not when
we were new and not

when I knew already his microbrew
sweat. He knocked
as I shat liquid,

cheeked linoleum, hushed
into kneecaps my song
to the landlord downstairs,

his chain smoke
seeping into my two good
thoughts. I took

Vicodin and my lover
wanted to go.
I slept alone,

woke to rock
on the mattress
and gawk the window

clean. It's tactile memory
I trust the most,
clasping the snow

of the tub's side.
In the pain break,
the smallest spiderwebs

behind the toilet,
easy and neutral
in their slight breeze,

so persistent
and completely separate.

Marcy Rae Henry

last payphone in times square

she came up to my eye.
i asked to borrow a pen.

people attend the removal of the
last payphone in times square.

i wrote her number in a note-
book stained into lines.

a power saw is used for the phone.
eulogies are said.

first time i called
set something in motion.

no one finds panegyrics to public
payphones unusual.

in my space we traded sketches.
hunger can be a project.

no one carries coins in pockets.
coins are an insult.

strawberries rotted in the fridge.
we woke each other up.

the fate of the phone is unknown.
museums have the best storage.

she gave me a piece of raw amber.
pine leather scents still intoxicate.

the last call was cinematic.
the end. as hollywood calls it.

Asia Calcagno

Searching Every One of My Former Ten Addresses on Google Maps

Somewhere, I am painting a wall marigold
and hanging bells on my doorknob. He is bending
me into the golden light of my apartment window
and I know the neighbors are watching.

Somewhere I pop the door open with one good
shove because this is a home where I do not own keys.
There is a place where I do not know the name
of the neighbors who gift poinsettias each December.

Somewhere, the neighborhood kids are watching
the pit bull birth and then swallow her babies whole.
A place where I cannot remember my age, but remember
I was young when I watched my father swallow the spider

eggs blooming in the corners of the porch. Somewhere
gravel pierces into the bottom of my feet like tiny teeth.
There are places where my mail is still being sent.
Places I cannot remember the exact address but know

the busy intersection or restaurants where we waited
in long lines for rib tips, the sweet aroma of hand car washes,
and the bitter tinge of gasoline. Somewhere, I learned how a
home will make you want to live longer and that every place

does not have to be my heartache. I learned that there are men
who will love you enough to drive the Uhaul, but the men who will
want to make love with you will pack your boxes and mop floors.
Somewhere I squeeze just enough furniture in a 6 x 8 living room.

Some places, I only own one knife, one Pyrex dish, and two
plates. I cook Thanksgiving dinners with one pan and one skillet.
Each night, I burn red candles that melt a waxy blood. Somewhere,
I am writing a check for late rent. A lover does not understand

why I always want to sleep at my place. Somewhere, the elderly
woman from upstairs is doing her nightly routine: she pours
fresh milk into a metal dish for the neighborhood cats and places
it in front of the abandoned building. It is now that I understand why.

—Nominated by *Third Coast Magazine*

nicole v basta

beside her unearthing

in the heavy country between
belonging to nowhere and clear off
pruned from the branch
a new moon and a stack of plates
rattle the night—even with these eyes
that could miss a whole future
scrubbing the dark, my hands delight
in the inconvenience
where we gather, wax from old candles
unsteadies our cups and mosquitoes sing
to our earrings while we eat
hard undoing says the woman who tends
the garden—she is glad to loosen
from the grip of what some have begun
to call progress
alfreda always wrist-deep beside her
unearthing what proves only ready now
we all commiserate about the water
-melon, too much shade makes
them never pinken
you can't move the sun i say
when i find old seeds in a pocket
i try to listen, i weigh them in my hands
i taste for the past

the woman tells us, *watch tonight, close*
the window she says
the rain will come thick
as milk

—Nominated by *Prism Review*

Lizabeth Yandel

Grocery Store, 12 a.m.

In aisle 5 I think maybe everybody hates
shopping for toilet paper like I hate
buying tampons & gasoline & soap. Nothing stays
full. I'm not required to restock but here I am,
living. I waste too much time
in the fancy appliance section because inside
I'm like the discount junk rack by the bathrooms
& I'm hoping no one will notice. You don't
go grocery shopping with me anymore. We eat
in different cities. You're probably slurping bland,
stupid noodles right now. A clerk asks if I'm ready
to check out. *No* I say *& aren't you sick of no one knowing*
what they want? He shrugs. Muzak-y music
twinkles overhead. I imagine he winks at me, gently
takes the plastic basket from my hand, slips the tank-top
strap off my shoulder. *Don't start* I would say *I need a donut.*
So, I take my basket to the bakery. The case is full of stale
apple fritters. I want to stuff them all into my cheeks
like a feral squirrel. But I can't afford love
handles, so I go to the deli to stare at bowls of weird
colorful salads. I know they are grosser than they look.
They're like you & you're like them, I think, *we all are.* I order
a quarter pound of some bean thing & head to self-checkout.
From the parking lot the stars are barely visible
& I remember they're mostly dead already. People are
amazed by this: starlight only reaches us postmortem.
& maybe that's not so different from our own pain,

synapses still firing in our brains lightyears after
the damage. It's like our neurotransmitters came late to the party,
the house now full of half-empty beer cups & a few drunk
people still trying to dance & I wander in like *hey guys*
but nobody notices, so I pick up a warm beer & drink
some & that song me & you used to dance to in the kitchen
comes on & the lyrics sound just like you lying to me
& I'm like *goddamn this song. Does anybody know*
this fucking song?   *Does anybody know it?!*

Poonam Dhir

Drawing from Old Currents

> *"As ordinary as it all appears,*
> *there are times when it is beyond my imagination."* —Jhumpa Lahiri, *Interpreter of Maladies*

My name: a mnemonic device. Pulled from the roots of a banyan tree. I am both epiphytic and a genderless bog. A woman at a kitchen sink. Washes her hands in an attempt to make decisions. Her life: a series of meals and overtime. Wanting a spine but receiving a prayer. Noctambulant bodies slink into pools. Wash peachy flesh until ripe with wonder.

Splitting violence to cross a border. Limbs become revolutions. Mechanisms for worship and rewards. Taking turns sorting attachments. Carving monuments out of buttered toast.

Weekend rituals,
promises held
in wax.

—Nominated by *Minola Review*

Miriam Alex

On the Reproduction of Images

"Images were first made to conjure up the appearances of something that was absent"
—John Berger

On the Reproduction of Images, Past

At the beginning of time,
before the sea and the single-celled,
was film. Every little moment
used to be everything to us—
clementines, basketed and bathing
in a pool of light, the gentle
ellipses of a robin's pale egg—
and nothing at all. When it was warm,
we couldn't remember the rain.
How could we? The light dim,
the camera ruined.

On the Reproduction of Images, Present

On your birthday, the neighbors
lounged in the kitchen. You poured
the tea; I shut the bedroom door,
our clothes piling like street dogs.
After, you say a little mess
is unimportant, and we argue. Later,
all I find dated on the day
of your mother's divorce is a vintage

stamp. A receipt for a toasted,
sesame bagel. A spot of jam
blooms at the corner of the paper,
purpling beneath the window.

I don't remember when we met,
just that we had. Sometimes, I wish
there was a love letter to name
the date, just to prove that it happened.
In the spring, I find another magazine
beneath your socks. The bodies
are pink, impossible. We fight again,
louder. Our anniversary leaks
through our hands. You blow out
the candle. We cut the cake.

On the Reproduction of Images, Future

Every autumn, you ask for a photo
of us, laughing over Niagara Falls.
Every year, we look like tourists,
our ponchos bright and yellow.

You never mind. This is enough
for you—the record will stay full,
never waning. *Look at that smile*,
you'll say, and I'll believe it every time.

On long days, I imagine a curator
writing about us. *The American Dream,*
the caption opens, *is to be in love.*

Windows down. Cheeks flushed.
The sky as blue as a robin's egg,
or hands left in the snow. *This*,
says the caption, *is everything one*
could want. How stupid we must have
looked. How loving, how happy.

Sam Niven

Solstice Poem

I get what I can at the local Piggly Wiggly: mushy strawberries, Blue Bell ice cream, shot glasses. At the beach, I pick up everything. Calico scallops, little empty bottles of Fireball. I'm learning to identify the Lady-in-Waiting Venus shell by its teeth. I'm learning the difference between seaworm shedding and a plastic straw wrapper. The leaves on the boardwalk turn out to be insects, camouflaged, flying away when I flip them over. The ocean gives me a sand dollar, dead, mostly whole, and half a pair of goggles. Broken currency of water. I walk up the coast for lightning whelks, down for banded tulips, rinsing everything in the tide, sprinkling baby powder to avoid sand in the house. My hands are chalky white and slippery and I have nothing to forgive. Today, I woke in time to watch the sun rise, the longest night behind me. I ate breakfast, drank bottled water without vodka, didn't stay up late making my own salt scrub. I'm letting the tide do that for me. I'm lying in the sand, hands over eyes, beside the top layer of a jellyfish, washed up from the ocean, dry as the moon. The redbreasted sunset doubles into the horizon: two strawberry scoops melting into one.

—Nominated by The Writing Seminars at Johns Hopkins University

Ian Cappelli

the frame of the stolen painting

carries the museum's wallpaper behind it. Your father constructs a scotch egg at your stepmother's house, with her kids. You both wear puffy jackets as you embrace. He wants you to be more stoic when he mocks a crowd of protesters. There are stubborn linen curtains in their guest room, thin windows. He is soft at his center. When waiters mishear your father's order, he starts to imitate their accents. He imitates your accent each time you argue. The fitted stones of the city are cold like a houseguest.

Parker Hobson

All Snakes' Day

For the violets left slain by the lawn guy.

For the rabbits who still guard the yard while we sleep.
For my grandfather's workshirt, clean

in my closet like the flag of a country
which no longer exists. For my cousin Ran, named forever

in the past tense. For *we're way past*
tents, we're in bungalows now, and for the baby snake that slipped
up through the floorboards of my terrible coalfield
home—It's like camping!
my landlord said—and for my friend Steven saying I thought about you
over there on the other side of the world,
did you hear I lost a son.

For the rockabilly postman, whose rolled cuffs hold
this town together. For the tide

of twilight, which might yet come to render
our brutalism beautiful. And for you, in your perfect rhombus

of winter-carpet sun, moving a finger
to your nose while you think—at first it was joke but it's grown
involuntary, like how I've started snorting since my friend
Jim died, like how I'm trying to repeat I love

this drop-tiled planet
with the whole of my heart until it's true.

antmen pimentel mendoza

Self-Portrait in a Canadian Tuxedo on the Road to St. George, Utah

Nothing is new, least of all a world. Empire
litters highways stretched through
a Vegas Costco Gas from a drive-up

Bakersfield ATM: Manifest
Destiny and her loveless slip of strip
malls and western hunger. She and her kin

in the afterlife flesh, roadside pastiche:
Looney Tunes tumbleweeds, settlers' namesakes
plaqued on stucco cum adobe, gift shops

in the shape of covered wagons, fascist
campaign slogans, my Lolo's face
I divine from the mountain.

I wear olive green boots. I can't button my jeans
as high up on my waist as I once did
and they tear in the places where thighs kiss.

Like my forefathers in vinegar-stained
shirtfronts before me, vulgar lidded
eyes crested on the mouth of a beer bottle,

the coil of time tightened fast in my shape.
I fold considering what it might mean
to know in the past tense, *I was here.*

Gauri Awasthi

Partition Story

No one moved. My very Hindu family did not leave the Gangetic plains because they haven't since uncountable generations and were not forced to. And his very Muslim family does not remember hearing much about the biggest migration. *We were so far north, it's almost Afghanistan.* When I was a child, I used to think I lived in the northernmost part of the whole entire world because my state is called Uttar Pradesh—*Uttar as in north, as in answer.* But no one moved. So, we stayed where we were. This is why my mother hates his mother. And his mother hates mine. If I bring his mother a rosy pink chikankari suit made from the hands of my favorite darzi in Lucknow, will she love my mother? If he brings the best biryani I've ever eaten to my mother's kitchen, made from the rice growing in Balochistan, will my mother agree to become his mother too? Because our mothers do not want to love each other, because we only love our mothers truly, we struggle to love each other. No one dies in this partition story, not immediately anyway. But we keep dying slowly. In our hometowns. In India and in Pakistan. While I keep running into British women telling me how to drink tea properly. *Yes, it is true that our kin were smashed like ants when your ancestors drew the goddamn line one morning* but instead, I just explain that lavender is my favorite flavor of herbal tea.

Matthew Tuckner

The Decline and Fall of the Roman Empire

Near the end of his life, the artist painted six coffins
egg-shell white, filling them with the cadavers

of diseased sea stars found in tidepools
along the coast of San Luis Obispo.

When we enter the gallery, you spill the contents
of your tote bag into a metal tray: camera lens, pill organizer,

a fragment of orange rind shaped like Florida,
a bottle of SmartWater, dyed gold with powdered electrolytes.

Only one canvas grabs your fleeting attention: abstract clots
of cloud, swirling with menace above a baby in a bassinet.

We know what's coming. We've been texting back and forth
famous last words as a way of making light of it,

a record of the mind speaking to the mind in dulcet tones,
reminding the mind it is still here, for now.

Heraclitus: *Can you turn wet water into dry?*
Caligula: *I am still very much alive.*

It appears that what will happen, hasn't happened yet.
So we fill the time with projects, Tokyo, memories

of its greedy koi fish, a ceramic bowl
of goji berries perfectly balanced on a tree branch.

We fatten the time until it bursts into artifacts:
sixteen photographs of a single puddle

taking shape in the red glow of your darkroom.
A puddle you glimpsed the moon in, & stopped for.

A puddle that was just plain rain until it fell.

Jim Whiteside

Caught the Bug

The museum is nearly empty

the day we visit the Mitchell retrospective.

We can wander, painting to painting.

He removes his blue-framed glasses, leaning close.

The modernists, he says, painted for the home,

not galleries. We should be viewing these pictures

seated in wingbacks. At ninety, he is my oldest friend.

At ninety, he's lost friends younger than me.

Last night, we sat in the room where his lover died,

drinking White Burgundy. He described seeing friends

on the sidewalk, men gone gaunt. Rushing by.

The last time he saw them alive.

You are like those friends, he said, *before*.

Others he could not describe—using a shorthand,

Caught the bug. On the end table, a ceramic sculpture

of a bull, fired with bright green glaze. Reaching out,

he touched its flank. Today, he stands in front

of an enormous painting. The rare emergence

of a figure. Green grass. A blue bird.

He is in the middle of a story about a great lunch,

years ago, with a beautiful man. *Caught the bug*, his story ends.

Turning away from me, facing the canvas.

Melissa McKinstry

Showering My Son

Now over one hundred pounds,
your soft body like the lead drape
a technician places before an x-ray.
Like Titian's *Venus of Urbino,* white and pink—
sans all that hair, sans the sentience in the eyes.
Every day for almost twenty-four years,
my arms under your shoulder blades and knees,
I scoop you out of bed, pivot you
to the blue-mesh chaise on wheels.
Your three stomata—a constellation
from throat to belly to bladder. Oh, the way
plastic meets the flesh. Our little mystery,
our science experiment, our boy. Let us
wheel to the shower now. I'll sluice warm
water over your chest, little tuft of hair.
I'll lift each arm and rinse your musky
man odor. I'll soap your groin, your legs,
and your rocker bottom feet with those
toes crossed for good luck. I'll shampoo
your hair, a sort of translucence. I'll shave
your chin, press a warm cloth gently
to each eye, the whorl of each ear,
the nape of your neck under the trach tie.
And then, the swaddle of towels,
the wheeling back to bed, and we'll
become *After the Bath* by Degas—
the hairbrush and the awkward limbs.

I'll lotion your knobby knees, thin shins,
each little finger that has never held
anything. I'll fluff your pillow,
cover you with your soft old blanket,
read you a poem. I'll be Frank O'Hara,
made for the lunchtime ritual of the city,
made for kangaroos, aspirins, beachheads, and biers.
"These things are with us every day," he says.
Made for the daily touch, for the reminder—
"You really are beautiful!" he says.

Regan Green

On Shaving

Hannah shaved
a nipple clean off
and claimed it grew back,
but no one could confirm this.
Ross had a light down that I loved
on his cheekbones
and which he shaved
just to spite me
after I won an argument
over whether god cares about art.
Noah lifted
his ponytail and asked me
to buzz the nape of his neck,
and this was more intimate
than the tender sex.
Rachel said the eyes
are the window to the soul,
and brows to the color of pubes.
We quickly hid
our faces from each other.
The first time I nicked the hard tendon
on the back of my knee with a new razor,
I watched the red run long and thin
for what felt like gallons,
thinking this is it,
this is how I go.
Who thinks of me when they shave?

I haven't shaved in a month.
Only I know the secret patch
of blond on my kneecap
that always eludes the razor.
Landen says that in my poetry
I cut at a subject
from several different angles.
I should try this approach on my knee.
Sometimes when I badly need
to shave, I have nightmares my leg hair
has grown long as cattails
under my church dress.
Scott's thick orange beard
exfoliated the skin around my mouth
when he kissed me.
Neely shaved during a layover
in the Tampa airport bathroom,
a leg propped up between sinks,
and women we didn't know
passed her foamed soap
in their cupped hands, saying
honey I hope he's worth it.

—Nominated by The Writing Seminars at Johns Hopkins University

Nicholas Yingling

The Anorexics Dream of Flight

I.

Imagine years of famine as a map
folded into our mothers' chromosomes:
a migration, a longing to winter

somewhere over the gulf. To better fly
songbirds gave up sweetness.
Imagine survival with only a taste

of milkweed in our prey: bitter, acrid
as all that wild brushland burning upwind.
Imagine the horizon as hunger.

Imagine the tongue as phantom pain.
Would we sing?

II.

Tomorrow we'll leave this city.
            We'll order the driest, whitest wines
by the flight and fill out
            the papers. Will you? I do.
And so on. And if the 405 is stopped dead by ten
            thousand painted ladies touching
our windshield—
            each a small blessing of oil—we'll take the 101.

Let the dying fill our vision
    with gold. We'll trust our own
migration. We too were born

under the old stars turning, the old combination
    locking us out
or in. Do you believe in space
    enough? To open wide
in full color
    a painted lady must digest itself first—heart, brain,
and all. I've heard it called a soup,
    my marrow. Soup,
cigarettes, black coffee, and speed lifted Dorothy
    forever out of Kansas and tomorrow
we'll click our heels and leave

this city an impression made of light,
    made heavier by its memory. Both.
It's okay, Love, to want both
    of everything. Two wings. Too much. To know
the widows under our lawn
    chairs and still sit, watching the sun set too
soon. We'll say, Let it
    burn, and never speak of calories.
We'll eat
    the fallout from honey, the plastic
from placenta. We'll eat forever

III.

chemicals straight from our bloodstreams
and if fire smokes the resin right
out of teeth, we'll shotgun the neighbors

into our folds. All stomach and cortex.
We'll bless the struggle to button up,
the years of exhaust

in our brainstems. Our heads
so marbled with matter, we'll see clearly
for miles and that aching blur between

your eyes will heal at last into four
years of my letters, which all begin the same:
Dear Sierra,

don't be afraid to stand,
there's so much atmosphere in your name.

IV.

And you can always drop
            it and be the middle Rose who loves our rich
earth for cleaning us like a child
            cleans their plate. And the child? Love,
maybe some adventures are just walking
            home. Picture it: an empty highway, poppies
nursing our ladies to sleep,
            maybe an apple
stand with two slices of pie. We won't have to
            share anything, the pavement
so full of lanes—could we ever really cross

together?

Helene Achanzar

O My Worry, I Reach for Your Hand

Scribbling on the back of this Medicaid mail
to the tune of a common tiredness. The cardboard

piling against the back door. I used to go places
like I was going places. The difference between outside

and inside when there is no door. For a time, the promise
of a cat in every bodega. These days, a rover landing

on Mars. I can sink my teeth into every lox bagel
and still fear the open sea. I once met a woman furious

about the perfume in Earl Grey. Threw an actual fit about it.
Could she imagine another world? Dating simulation games

and Texas strung out with snow. For three weeks
my sedan buried in ice. Thaw will render it a boat.

So I ordered two pairs of hiking boots—one for myself,
and one for myself when I'm feeling brave.

—Nominated by *Georgia Review*

Jackson Holbert

After C.D. Wright

I need a curtain and some lemonade,
spiders for friends, and a nice

lawn to have my visions on. I should
have never let that church buy my father's

piano for slightly under market value.
I should have taken the contents

of my mother's fridge when I had the chance.
I would be thin no longer nor young

if I had done the things I should have done.
If the best among the least of all the trees

I planted long ago to brace
the hillsides against strong rain

still stand after this spring, I'll fill my best glass
with water, and put on a little music.

Monica Rico

Five Things Borrowed

—after Sandra Cisneros

I wanted to   and did leave Saginaw.
My Spanish is
concealed
because   I ask too much from
the smell
of lemons.
I am the woman who
didn't take

her husband's name, or

have children.

No one   wonders when
I will grow a vegetable garden
or if

I liked New York. I have

not changed my

phone number
in twenty years.
When the daffodils bloom

I bring them inside.

I have yet to see

a person along the Huron River
lost in bird song
waiting to return
to sky.

I grew up
with the privilege
of   a   father
who looks
exactly   like me
and   I learned   the most
from dishwashing

when my brother's wife ran off to Jamaica

when she came back
my mother-in-law wanted to teach me

the correct way
to wash her son's shirts.
The last time
I was a ring
was after a party
everyone home and apron
around my neck. The time I heard the geese
traveling with the moon
I believed I was hallucinating and now when they wake me
I know I'm not and imagine I am
an owl falling swiftly
on the sound.

Hannah Smith

Armadillo

Their bloated bodies line the highways
close to home. I've never seen one alive
trudging across sandy soil, tail mirrored in the length
of its own snout. I find them feet-up, tail-down, head severed

on another part of road. My father tells me,
armadillos carry leprosy. We must've learned not to touch them
when we were young and running in the tall grass
of cattle country. In Leviticus, someone told Moses

to clean the dead with two live birds, cedar, and hyssop—
a flowering herb so akin to bluebonnets, I question which plant
is inked on my ankle. Centuries later in a land
not their own, on a failed mission for salvation,

crusaders carried lepronic lesions and gangrene, skeletal
frames beneath chain link and breast plates. One
of their kings, sick himself, could not bring his body
even to blink. He died blind, his eyes dry and wide,

staring into the heat of the desert. I hold cow parsley
close to my chest, take in another quiet, hot field.
Someone paid twice the asking price for soil
that grows nothing but weeds. It's a wonder

any critter lives here, even one so armored. I shove
my feet into boots ankle-deep, grind up the dirt
with my heels, root myself into this expanse that was
never mine. I place my weeds in a vase of clean water.

—Nominated by The Ohio State MFA Program

Alejandro Lucero

Busted Pandemic Sonnet for My Dead Dad

You taught me how to touch you like a house
of cards. Focus my breath away from the tilt

of your neck. They painted the coils of a ram’s horns tar heel blue
for that last football game we saw. The fuzzy picture dying

to fade away. The way you hit ~~the hard side of our t.v.~~
made me flinch. But it worked, didn’t it? That “love

tap.” You saved every receipt. Desk drawers stuffed with evidence
of all you spent on razor blades ~~never used~~. I barely saw your hair

under that Broncos cap, until you asked me
to cut it all off. *Leave the beard*, you told me, rusted clippers humming

too close to your cheek. I bought another box
of fifty masks today, Tar Heel blue. (You’ve missed so much

bullshit). Men on ESPN say we shouldn’t wear them; cosmetic as painting ~~that alpha~~
~~-keratin we can’t shed.~~ Cheers, to you, Dad, for not covering your hairy mouth

~~when I kissed you goodbye.~~

—Nominated by Quarterly West

Will Goodwin

The Music in My Airpods Is Non-Diegetic

Barb and I went to the cemetery—to Oak Hill Cemetery

Where it was a sodden day

and we took mushrooms at Oak Hill and walked down separate paths

that wound through the headstones

and as I came up

on a path on one of the steep upper grades

the ground began the familiar breathing and

the sky rounded off and the sky became the firmament

and I was back on Cyprus Avenue

where I leaned against a railing

and felt the late morning

verging on saying something to me,

what it always verges on saying, but never says, or always says, but never comes close,

what the day verges on saying when the shadows are least

(when Pan might be glimpsed)

and as it didn't say something

and as all the mossy little towns

were bustling below me

I noticed a woman in a gazebo with her face in her lap.

She wore a green shirt.

I couldn't remember what Barb had worn.

The woman in the gazebo was crying.

I wished I could call out to her but

I wished I was

stepping into a quiet street

in a whaling town

looking so heroic in my long coat

with my long shadow

lowering myself into the barroom

to drink

with truckers and the kickers and the cowboy angels

to drink with the triggermen

and whisper of disavowed movements

and watch a knife fight in the alley

and put my hand on a good man's chest and say, "Don't stop them, they're right."

But I was just wearing my comfy jeans

and the woman in the gazebo was crying.

I wished desperately that I could call out to her

I wanted nothing more than that

but it would have been impossible

and I don't need to explain why.

There was nothing I could do for the woman.

I hated that.

Then, when she turned around,

streaky-faced and blubbering,

I was so relieved

The woman couldn't have been crying,

because it was Barb,

and Barb and I were having a lovely day.

Juliana Chang

The Most Taiwanese Thing about Me

—after Katie Mansfield

not the tub of bean curd in my freezer.
not the Lao Gan Ma chili oil
I drink by the spoonful like my Ba.
not how I fish pork blood out of my soup
to drop into my brother's bowl,
not any acre of my mouth, really.

not my two passports
or my two names.
not the yearbook photo retake
that made twins of me in second grade,
Ting Wei and Juliana printed out
side by side. not the time I made Kevin cry
telling him Chang is a better last name
than Zhang.

not my ninth Halloween.
not when I asked my Ma for jack-o'-lanterns
and she scratched smiley faces into the pumpkins
with a butter knife.
not the way my Ma pronounces *butter*, or *knife,*
          or *library*—not the *li-barry*, the Ikea bag of books,
the sofa cushions that ate a paperback each month.

instead, just the way my Ma hugs at airports.
last time I saw her, she squeezed so hard
I thought she was trying to seal me
back inside my body.
I didn't know I was an island
until then.

Laura Cresté

Egg Party

The spring my systems go wrong, I throw a party
where the theme is eggs. Chicken eggs deviled

and overburdened. Caviar held precariously
to potato chip by a slick of cream.

The idea is rebirth, claim whatever rituals
remain palatable. Spring of resisting

augury, not interpreting what it means
that one part of my body wants

to kill another part. In the dark
socket of jar, the black roe teem.

Some people are nauseated by clusters:
a shucked pomegranate disclosing its cells,

studded face of a sunflower enough to swoon.
That's not what makes me sick. I spoon,

I scratch the blood from boiled egg halves
with a fingernail. I am now buzzing

with terrible purpose: white blood cells
assemble in my throat, like a swarm

of ants taking down larger prey;
I'll be obvious and picture a butterfly,

the thyroid always described as a winged gland.
Meanwhile, I go on chopping dill and tapping

eggs open against the sink. My friend, a twin, helps peel—
cracks a double-yolk and misses her sister.

This spring, in the forest, a small bird hooked onto my palm
with devastating trust. Two sunflower seeds slotted into her beak

as I fit into my life, almost comfortably,
almost equal to the task, the daily braveries required.

At the party where no one is heartbroken, there's a touching
fidelity to theme. The florals and golds. The small wants.

Egg whites fizzing the whiskey in our cups.
The possible fish popping against teeth.

Martha Paz-Soldan

Carmen Amaya

(1913–1963)

I.

The children watch through the bullet
holes in the walls of the bar my lover

on the guitar, singing about a church
that goes up in flames. I quicken the footwork

until I'm cutting through a wheatfield
like a runaway bride. I want to make it

unmistakable—hands torquing
like shot-down birds, a litany of knuckles

rapping on the table—the sound
of a woman getting away with it.

II.

Every day in Somorrostro, my sisters and I
watched the tide come in closer and closer.

When no one was looking, the water
would pool into our *barracos* up to our ankles.

This is a cautionary tale but without the lesson,
just men from the city who arrive with axes,

who look right past you after they finish
knocking down the neighbor's house.

III.
In the matador's suit, I abandon all heroics.
I break through the floorboards, sidestepping

an animal made visible by each leap
in the air, my barricade of hair falling

from the updo. There's valor
in a horn to the heart, just no music.

IV.
In the movies, I wear the face of a girl
who's spat out blood before. I have stopped

begging for change, but the body goes
where the mind cannot follow. My father

ten years younger, in his best suit,
his hand striking his guitar so furiously

his nail flies clean off. The police storming
the tavern in search of a girl too young

to be dancing but small enough for a stranger
to hide in his bargain coat. We walk down

the street, two sets of legs to one shadow,
pretending we're something we're not.

Meg Reynolds

Discipline

I watch nature documentaries in the morning.
Rain in the Scottish Highlands, mist lifting

from a capercaillie's croaking throat. He
is swollen, massive with want and fight,
buoyant as a heart. Vermillion

stripes over his eyes, the fan
of his body expanding

and contracting against the grasses
beneath the pines. Look
how close you are to me still,

slick on his feathers, rising from his call.
We've been through this, all I wanted

to teach you, a love affair with the earth
I brought you to. Wonder is a discipline
I wanted you to be good at.

Then was I going to teach you how to speak.
Your father was going to teach you how

to garden, fat green beans and marigolds.
We were going to be careful with how you
handled the cat. When I wept in the dim room

during the third ultrasound, the one
that revealed your death,

it was in loneliness. How did you
handle it so deftly, so completely?
My children, that you would

do something like dying without me
to guide you. You,
my dark fists opening.

—Nominated by *ARTS & LETTERS*

Greg Nicholl

Sage

I said I'd see the fire safely extinguished
even though we finished the last beer
hours ago. I told you it was jet lag, but to be alone
in the backyard of a town not mine was all
I wanted that evening. To pretend the bodies
asleep upstairs were mine to protect.
The fire pit. The orange plastic chairs.
The picnic table where we reunited over steak
and stories, your youngest demanding I sit
next to her on the bench, giggling when
I mispronounced *schwül.* It's an honest mistake.
The difference between gay and humid. And I
am always a little bit both. After dinner,
we walked the garden border and I quizzed her
on names of herbs, even though I momentarily
forgot the word for *sage.* Together we tore corners
off *Petersilie* and *Bärlauch,* touched them
to our tongues while you watched, skeptical
that the tiny shoots we plucked were indeed edible.
I liked sharing this with her. Being this. Someone
she will never see again, but may remember.
In the morning, you quietly watched from the corner
of the kitchen as we ate breakfast at the counter
and she showed me her workbook, of the cartoon
German boys and girls, who were any boy and girl.
And I can't remember if I told you last night how I,
myself, was almost a father, how the mother decided

to keep her. That I respected this and at the same time
broke. When it was time for us to go our separate
directions, I smiled as I heard her whispering
to herself while she packed her school bag:
Salbei, Rosmarin. Lorbeer. Erdbeer. Himbeer.

Joseph R. Chaney

Riches

When my grandfather came back from the dead
odd things thrilled him. He laughed at the faucet.
"All the bubbles!" he said, "I remember!"
He drank: "Water tastes like something. It's not
empty. It has flavor!" He'd want to launch
his boat in the sink, so I dragged him out
to the backyard where the trees were blooming,
and, oh boy, he was jumping up and down.
I tried to calm him. All the full blossoms!
The green! He knelt and bowed, eyes closed, and pressed
his face to the grass. He drew one long breath,
filling himself with earth's smells. So little
did he feel that he was owed anything,
or could repay the riches of a life.

Dāshaun Washington

A Fairy Tale of Blackboyhood

When I say *Black,* what I mean is the curl of my hair is tight enough to snag the teeth of a wide-tooth comb. So, I don't comb my hair when I'm in the comfort of my home. This comfort is the standard by which I determine who, what, where is home. I rarely feel home in my father's home.

*

When I was twenty-one, my father kissed my forehead and this was the first time he ever kissed me. My father's lips recall a different story. But this is my tale of a boy whose hard head grew tender from his father's kiss. The words *I love you boy* seeped into my newly-softened skull. For just a moment, my father returned my boyhood so he could feel the gratification of kissing his son goodnight. It had to be that way.

*

The only way to rake my hair into a neat brush of manageable coils is to first wet it thoroughly. Before I leave my home, I sometimes—most times—tame my hair with water to allow it to floss the teeth of the comb, to bear the brunt of its bite. I sometimes long for watered-down brown tresses that know to bow to the comb's might. I sometimes wish my hair would grow into an impenetrable forest, endless and black as starless nights.

*

When I say *Black*, I mean my father's hardened bosom has left me disheartened—desensitized to all but the snatch of a fine-tooth comb. I've been taught a man must be made a boy before he can receive a kiss from another man, and such ancient magic must be sparingly used. Sometimes—most times—I sleep with one eye open and hope to reunite with the strange magician who makes boys of men with forehead kisses. On these nights, I lie in bed and wait for him to cast his spell. As I sleep, my father combs his fingers through my hair and plants his lips on my eager forehead. On these nights, I wake floating above my bed in boyish bliss. On these nights, I feel home.

Acknowledgments

Helene Achanzar's "O My Worry, I Reach for Your Hand" previously appeared in *Georgia Review.*

Luciana Arbus-Scandiffio's "Index of Me" previously appeared in *Washington Square Review.*

nicole v basta's "beside her unearthing" previously appeared in *Prism Review.*

Tina Blade's "Vine Maple" previously appeared in *Apple Valley Review.*

Anthony Borruso's "Murphy's Law" previously appeared in *Aquifer: The Florida Review Online.*

Asia Calcagno's "Searching Every One of My Former Ten Addresses on Google Maps" previously appeared in *Third Coast Magazine.*

Ian Cappelli's "the frame of the stolen painting" previously appeared in *Greensboro Review.*

Juliana Chang's "The Most Taiwanese Thing about Me" previously appeared in *Hayden's Ferry Review.*

Laura Cresté's "Egg Party" previously appeared in *The Cortland Review.*

Poonam Dhir's "Drawing from Old Currents" previously appeared in *Minola Review.*

Ira Goga's "Faggots" previously appeared in *DIALOGIST.*

Marcy Rae Henry's "last payphone in times square" previously appeared in *Mud Season Review.*

Lina Herman's "Before We Rushed Our Daughter to the Hospital" previously appeared in *New Ohio Review.*

Jackson Holbert's "After C.D. Wright" previously appeared in *West Branch.*

Jasmine Khaliq's "Ghazal for My Father" previously appeared in *RHINO.*

Anthony Thomas Lombardi's "speed trap town" previously appeared in *Up the Staircase Quarterly.*

Alejandro Lucero's "Busted Pandemic Sonnet for My Dead Dad" previously appeared in *Quarterly West.*

Melissa McKinstry's "Showering My Son" previously appeared in *Beloit Poetry Journal.*

Alicia Rebecca Myers's "G-Day" previously appeared in *the arts fuse.*

Greg Nicholl's "Sage" previously appeared in *Nimrod.*

antmen pimentel mendoza's "Self-Portrait in a Canadian Tuxedo on the Road to St. George, Utah" previously appeared in *Split Lip Magazine.*

Pablo Piñero Stillmann's "Present" previously appeared in *Gettysburg Review.*

Meg Reynolds's "Discipline" previously appeared in *ARTS & LETTERS* and in *Does the Earth.*

Monica Rico's "Five Things Borrowed" previously appeared in *Wildness.*

Caitlin Roach's "Washington" previously appeared in *Narrative.*

Samyak Shertok's "Love in a Time of Revolution" previously appeared in *The Iowa Review.*

Hannah Smith's "Armadillo" previously appeared in *Superstition Review.*

Matthew Tuckner's "The Decline and Fall of the Roman Empire" previously appeared in *The Adroit Journal.*

Alice White's "Multiple Choice" previously appeared in *Black Warrior Review.*

Jim Whiteside's "Caught the Bug" previously appeared in *Ploughshares.*

Contributors' Notes

Helene Achanzar is a poet and editor whose writing has appeared in *Oxford American*, *Sixth Finch*, *Georgia Review*, and elsewhere. Winner of the 2022 New England Review Award for Emerging Writers, she is a senior editor for *Poetry Northwest*, Midwest regional chair for Kundiman, and director of programs at the Chicago Poetry Center.

Miriam Alex is from southern New Hampshire. Her work is published or forthcoming in *Frontier Poetry*, *Gigantic Sequins*, *Gone Lawn*, and *Uncanny Magazine*. In 2021, she was one of New Hampshire's Youth Poet Laureates.

Emily Alexander is from Idaho. Her poetry has been published in journals such as *Narrative*, *Penn Review*, and *Conduit*, and she has written for *The Inlander* and *Literary Hub*. She works in restaurants and lives in Brooklyn.

Luciana Arbus-Scandiffio is a Wallace Stegner Fellow at Stanford University. She is a graduate of the Michener Center for Writers in Austin, Texas, where she was a recipient of the Fania Kruger Fellowship. Her poems have appeared or are forthcoming in *Bennington Review*, *Greensboro Review*, *Southern Indiana Review*, and *Copenhagen*. Luci has two lesbian moms and is originally from New Jersey.

Gauri Awasthi, born and raised in Kanpur, India, received her MFA in creative writing from McNeese State University. Her work explores the themes of origin, grief, and borders embedded in the figure of her elders. She has won fellowships from Yaddo, Bread Loaf Writers' Conference, Sundress Academy for The Arts, Hambidge Center for Creative Arts and Sciences, Hedgebrook, and Louisiana Office of Cultural Development. Her writing has been published in *Quarterly West*, *Notre Dame Review*, *The Wire*, *Buzzfeed*, *Provincetown Arts Magazine*, and others. She is an associate editor at *The Offing* and runs the Decolonizing Poetry Workshop.

NICOLE V BASTA is a poet, educator, visual artist, vintage seller, arts showcase curator, enthusiastic collaborator, and scrappy, wandering weirdo proudly descended from Pennsylvania coal miners and garment factory workers. Recent poems have found homes in *Ploughshares*, *Waxwing*, *Plume*, *RHINO*, *North American Review*, *The Cortland Review*, and elsewhere. She is the author of the chapbook *V* (2017), winner of The New School's Annual Contest, and the chapbook *the next field over* (2022), from Tolsun Books. For more, see nicolevbasta.com.

TINA BLADE is a Pushcart Prize and Best of the Net nominee. Her poems have appeared in *The Moth*, *Apple Valley Review*, *Sweet Tree Review*, *Calyx*, *Seattle Review*, *Bracken*, and elsewhere. A lifelong resident of the Pacific Northwest, she holds an MFA in poetry from the University of Oregon and currently lives in Duvall, Washington, just east of Seattle.

ANTHONY BORRUSO is PhD candidate in creative writing at Florida State University where he is a poetry editor for *Southeast Review*. He has been a host for the Jerome Stern Reading Series and was selected as a finalist for *Beloit Poetry Journal*'s Adrienne Rich Award by Natasha Trethewey. His poems have been published or are forthcoming in *Denver Quarterly*, *Beloit Poetry Journal*, *Pleiades*, *The Cincinnati Review*, *The Journal*, *THRUSH*, *Gulf Coast*, *CutBank*, *Frontier*, and elsewhere.

CHRISTINE BYRNE is a writer from Connecticut. She is currently an MFA candidate at the Iowa Writers' Workshop, where she won the John Logan Poetry Prize. Her most recent work is forthcoming from the *New England Review*, *Sugar House Review*, *The Journal*, and elsewhere.

ASIA CALCAGNO is a writer and educator from Chicago. Her work has been published in *Third Coast*, *Poetry*, *Black Femme Collective*, *The Golden Shovel Anthology*, *Smartish Pace*, and various other journals and anthologies. Asia holds an MFA from Bennington College and was selected as a 2022 Luminarts Creative Writing Fellow.

IAN CAPPELLI is a creative writing (poetry) PhD student at the University of Denver. He received his MFA from George Mason University, where he was awarded the 2021 MFA Thesis Fellowship in Poetry. His work has recently appeared, or is forthcoming, in

The Iowa Review, *West Branch*, *RHINO*, *Lake Effect*, *Atlanta Review*, *The Journal*, *Sugar House Review*, *Terrain*, and *Palette Poetry*, among others.

Joseph R. Chaney's poetry has appeared in many journals, including *The Nation*, *Prairie Schooner*, *Crazyhorse*, *Yankee*, *Black Warrior Review*, *Beloit Poetry Journal*, *Spillway*, *Valparaiso Poetry Review*, *South Florida Poetry Journal*, *Wisconsin Review*, *Apple Valley Review*, and the *Journal of Humanistic Mathematics*. He was born in Illinois and grew up in California, Georgia, and Tennessee. He attended Berea College before transferring to Beloit College, where he won the Academy of American Poets Prize. He completed his graduate work at the University of California, Irvine. Chaney was a Fulbright Fellow at the Chinese University of Hong Kong. He teaches writing and literature at Indiana University South Bend, where he directs Wolfson Press.

Juliana Chang is a Taiwanese-American poet. Her debut poetry chapbook, *INHERITANCE*, was the winner of the 2020 Vella Prize. Juliana's work appears or is forthcoming in *The American Poetry Review*, *The Chestnut Review*, *diode poetry journal*, *Burningword Literary Magazine*, and other publications. She holds a BA in linguistics, an MA in sociology from Stanford University, and is currently a student at Harvard Law School.

Laura Cresté is the author of the chapbook *You Should Feel Bad*, which won a 2019 Chapbook Fellowship from the Poetry Society of America. Her work has appeared in *The American Poetry Review*, *Bennington Review*, *The Cortland Review*, *The Kenyon Review*, *Poetry Northwest*, *The Yale Review*, and elsewhere. She holds an MFA from New York University and was a 2021–2022 Writing Fellow at the Fine Arts Work Center, in Provincetown, Massachusetts. The recipient of an emerging artist grant from the St. Botolph Club Foundation, she has received fellowships, scholarships, and residencies from Monson Arts, the Sewanee Writers' Conference, the Tin House Summer Workshop, and the Community of Writers.

Poonam Dhir is a queer poet, playwright, Punjabi descendent, and settler currently based in Tiohtiá:ke (Montréal), on the traditional, unceded territory of the Kanien'kehá:ka people. They are the recipient of a 2022 Lambda Literary Fellowship in Playwriting and a finalist for the 2021 PEN Canada New Voices Award, Poetry. They are an Artist-in-Residence at Infinithéâtre. You can read her latest pieces in *The Capilano Review*, *Vallum*, *Minola Review*, *Contemporary Verse 2*, and *PRISM International*. Find Poonam online @pnmdhir.

María Esquinca is a poet and journalist. A fronteriza, she was born in Ciudad Juárez, Chihuahua, Mexico and grew up in El Paso, Texas. Her poetry has appeared in *Waxwing*, *The Florida Review*, *Glass: A Journal of Poetry*, *Scalawag*, *Acentos Review*, and *No Tender Fences: An Anthology of Immigrant & First-Generation American Poetry*. In 2018, she won the Alfred Boas Poetry Prize from the Academy of American Poets judged by Victoria Chang. Her book reviews and interviews have appeared in *Adroit Journal* and *ANMLY*.

Ira Goga is a trans poet and biochemist whose work has been published in *The Adroit Journal*, *DIAGRAM*, *Foglifter*, and elsewhere. They have received support from the Ucross Foundation and the Academy of American Poets. They currently live in Austin, Texas, where they are pursuing an MFA.

Will Goodwin is originally from North Carolina. He writes about alienation, spiritual esotericism, the surveillance state, and wildlife. He is an ordained minister, a scuba diver, and a competent singer. He received his MFA in nonfiction from NYU in 2023. He is writing his first novel. He can be found at willgoodwin.substack.com.

Regan Green grew up in Tennessee and lives in Baltimore, where she is a junior lecturer in the Writing Seminars at Johns Hopkins University. She is the assistant editor of the *Birmingham Poetry Review*, and other poems of hers are forthcoming in the *Southern Poetry Anthology: Volume X*.

Julian Guy is a queer and trans writer and educator currently residing in Syracuse, New York. A 2023 Tin House Scholar, his poems have been published in *swamp pink*, *Catapult*, *The Adroit Journal*, *the winnow*, *Dinner Bell Magazine*, *Queerlings Magazine*, and more. A nonfiction editor for *Variant Literature* and a 2021 Brooklyn Poets Staff Pick, Julian teaches advanced poetry classes through Ellipsis Writing on the intersections of mutual aid, poetry, and community. Find Julian online at his website, julianguy.com, or at the beach plucking oysters up from the seafoam.

Marcy Rae Henry es una Latina/e de Los Borderlands. Her writing has received a Chicago Community Arts Assistance Grant, an Illinois Arts Council Fellowship, a Pushcart Prize nomination and first prize in *Suburbia Journal*'s 2021 Novel Excerpt Contest. Writing and visual art appear in *The Worcester Review*, *Waxwing*, *PANK*, *The Southern Review*, *The Glacier*, and *The Brooklyn Review*, among others. M.R. Henry is an associate professor of literature and creative writing at Wright College, an editor for *RHINO*, and a digital minimalist with no social media accounts. For more, see marcyraehenry.com.

Lina Herman is a poet and writer living in California. Her work has appeared or is forthcoming in *New Ohio Review*, *Salt Hill Journal*, and *BOOTH*, among others. For more, please visit linaherman.com.

Parker Hobson is a poet from Louisville, Kentucky, whose work has also appeared in *32 Poems*, *Denver Quarterly*, *Best New Poets 2019*, *Conduit*, *Poetry Daily*, and elsewhere. He graduated in 2018 from the University of Kentucky's MFA Program in Creative Writing, and he currently works as a producer of radio stories for Appalshop, a non-profit media arts center serving the Appalachian Mountains of East Kentucky. He is also a songwriter, and his newest record, *Loss Program*, is forthcoming in 2024.

Jackson Holbert was born and raised in eastern Washington and currently lives in Oakland, where he is a Jones Lecturer at Stanford. His first book, *Winter Stranger* (Milkweed Editions), won the Max Ritvo Prize. His work has appeared in *The Iowa Review*, *The Nation*, and *Poetry*.

Jasmine Khaliq is a Pakistani Mexican American poet born and raised in Northern California. Her work is found or forthcoming in *Poetry Northwest*, *Poet Lore*, *The Rumpus*, *Bennington Review*, *Cincinnati Review*, and elsewhere. She holds an MFA from University of Washington, Seattle. Currently, Jasmine is a PhD student at the University of Utah, where she teaches and serves as editor for *Quarterly West*. She can be found at jasminekhaliq.com.

Anthony Thomas Lombardi is the author of *Murmurations* (YesYes Books, 2025), a 2021–2022 Poetry Project Emerge—Surface—Be Fellow, and a multiple Pushcart Prize and Best of the Net nominee, among other accolades. He has taught or continues to teach with Borough of Manhattan Community College, Paris College of Art, Brooklyn Poets, *Polyphony Lit*'s apprenticeship programs, community programming throughout New York City, and currently serves as a poetry editor for *Sundog Lit*. His work has appeared or is forthcoming in *Guernica*, *Black Warrior Review*, *Narrative Magazine*, *Colorado Review*, *Thrush Poetry Journal*, the Poetry Foundation website, and elsewhere. He lives in Brooklyn with his wife and their two cats.

Alejandro Lucero's chapbook, *Sapello Son*, was named the Editors' Selection for the 2022 Frost Place Competition and is forthcoming with Bull City Press. His latest work appears/is forthcoming in *The Cincinnati Review*, *Cream City Review*, *The Florida Review*, *RHINO*, and *The Southern Review*. An MFA student in the Writing Seminars at Johns Hopkins University, he lives in Baltimore and serves as an assistant editor for *The Hopkins Review*.

Nick Martino is a poet and teacher from Milwaukee, Wisconsin. His work is published or forthcoming from *The Southern Review*, *Narrative*, *Blackbird*, *The Los Angeles Review*, and *West Branch*, among others. He holds an MFA from the University of California, Irvine and was the winner of the program's 2022 Excellence in Poetry Prize. He lives in Los Angeles.

Melissa McKinstry holds an MFA from Pacific University. Her poems have been nominated for Best of the Net, a Pushcart Prize, and appear in journals including *Rattle*, *Alaska Quarterly Review*, *december*, *Tahoma Literary Review*, *SWWIM*, *Nimrod International*, and *Beloit Poetry Journal*. For more, please visit MelissaMcKinstry.com.

Alicia Rebecca Myers's poems and essays have appeared in *Creative Nonfiction*, *FIELD*, *Gulf Coast*, *SWWIM*, *december*, *Threadcount*, and *The Rumpus*. Her first full-length manuscript was a finalist for the 2023 Akron Poetry Prize, and her chapbook of poems, *My Seaborgium* (Brain Mill Press), was winner of the inaugural Mineral Point Chapbook Series. She lives with her husband and son in upstate New York.

Greg Nicholl is a freelance editor whose poetry has appeared or is forthcoming in *Gulf Coast, New Ohio Review, Nimrod, North American Review, River Styx, Smartish Pace, Sugar House Review, West Branch,* and elsewhere. He is the winner of the 2021 River Styx International Poetry Contest selected by Adrian Matejka and was a finalist for the 2022 Pablo Neruda Prize for Poetry from *Nimrod.*

Sam Niven is an MFA student in the Writing Seminars at Johns Hopkins University. They received the Elizabeth K. Moser Fellowship in Poetry Studies in 2023 and the Ethel Lowry Handley Prize from the Academy of American Poets in 2021. Sam lives in Baltimore with their partner, two cats, and thirty-nine houseplants.

Martha Paz-Soldan is a Peruvian American poet from South Florida. She is currently an MFA candidate in poetry at the University of Michigan's Helen Zell Writers' Program. She was named a finalist in *Narrative*'s Fifteenth Annual Poetry Contest and won a University of Michigan Hopwood Graduate Poetry Award in 2023.

antmen pimentel mendoza (she, he, they) is the author of the chapbook *MY BOYFRIEND APOCALYPSE* (Nomadic Press, 2023). antmen is a writer, the interim director of the Multicultural Community Center at UC Berkeley, and a student at the Rainier Writing Workshop at Pacific Lutheran University. His poetry is published or forthcoming in *Underblong, Peach Mag, A Velvet Giant,* and *Split Lip Magazine.* Find antmen online at @antmenismagic and antmenpm.com or riding her bike in Oakland, California.

Pablo Piñero Stillmann has been the recipient of Mexico's two top grants for young writers: The Foundation for Mexican Literature (f,l,m) and The National Fund for Culture and Arts (FONCA). His work has appeared in, among other places, *Bennington Review, Gettysburg Review, Mississippi Review,* and *Blackbird.* His book of short stories *Our Brains and the Brains of Miniature Sharks* won the Moon City Short Fiction Award and was published in 2020 by Moon City Press.

Annie P. Quigley is a writer, editor, and poet. She was named as one of ten finalists in *Fugue*'s 2021 Writing Contest and recently completed work on her first manuscript of poetry as part of Catapult's year-long intensive with the poet Angel Nafis. By day, Annie is the editor of the design publication *Remodelista* and authored the book *Remodelista in Maine: A Design Lover's Guide to Inspired, Down-to-Earth Style* (Artisan Books, 2022). She lives in Maine.

Meg Reynolds is a poet, artist, and teacher from New England. An instructor in writing and humanities at Vermont Adult Learning in Burlington, her work has been published in a number of literary journals including *Mid-American Review*, *RHINO*, *The Offing*, *Iterant*, *Prairie Schooner*, *New England Review*, and *The Kenyon Review*. A graduate of the Stonecoast MFA Program, her poetry and comic work has been twice nominated for the Pushcart Prize and once for Best the Net. Her first collection of poetry comics, *A Comic Year*, was published in October 2021 from Finishing Line Press. Her second collection, *Does the Earth*, was published in May 2023 from Harpoon Books.

Monica Rico is Mexican American and the author of *PINION*, winner of the Four Way Books Levis Prize in Poetry selected by Kaveh Akbar. She holds an MFA from the University of Michigan's Helen Zell Writers' Program and is the program manager for the Bear River Writers' Conference. She has published poems in *The Atlantic*, The Academy of American Poets' *Poem-A-Day*, *The Slowdown*, *Ecotone*, *The Nation*, and *Gastronomica*. Follow her at monicaricopoet.com.

Caitlin Roach earned an MFA in poetry from the Iowa Writers' Workshop. A three-time National Poetry Series finalist, her work has received prizes and recognition from the 92NY's Discovery Poetry Contest, the W.B. Yeats Society of New York for the Yeats Poetry Prize, *Narrative*'s fifteenth and tenth Annual Poetry Contests, and the International Literary Awards Rita Dove Award in Poetry, among others. Her poems appear in *Best New Poets 2021* and 2017, *jubilat*, *Narrative Magazine*, *Tin House*, *The Iowa Review*, *Poetry Daily*, *Denver Quarterly*, *Colorado Review*, *Columbia Journal*, and *Poetry Northwest*, among other publications. Her poem "Washington" was awarded Finalist in *Narrative*'s Fifteenth Annual Poetry Contest. She lives in the Pacific Northwest with her husband and their two sons.

Dennison Ty Schultz is a queer poet from Arkansas, currently living in Kansas with their partner and miniature poodle. They hold an MFA from the University of Missouri–

Kansas City. Their work has appeared in *Foglifter*, *Sycamore Review*, *New Delta Review*, *Black Warrior Review*, *Split Lip Magazine*, *Ninth Letter*, and *DIAGRAM*, among others. They tweet @clubdenni.

Samyak Shertok's poems appear or are forthcoming in *Poetry*, *The Cincinnati Review*, *The Gettysburg Review*, *Gulf Coast*, *The Iowa Review*, *The Kenyon Review*, *New England Review*, *Best New Poets*, and elsewhere. A finalist for the National Poetry Series, the Agnes Lynch Starrett Poetry Prize, and the Jake Adam York Prize, he has received fellowships from Aspen Words, the Helene Wurlitzer Foundation, and the Fine Arts Work Center in Provincetown. His work has been awarded the Robert and Adele Schiff Award for Poetry, the Gulf Coast Prize in Poetry, and the Auburn Witness Poetry Prize. Originally from Nepal, he holds a PhD in literature and creative writing from the University of Utah and is currently the inaugural Hughes Fellow in Poetry at Southern Methodist University.

Aurora Shimshak grew up in several rural communities in Wisconsin. Her poetry has appeared in *Poetry Northwest*, *New Ohio Review*, and *The Offing*, among others. She holds an MFA in poetry from University of Wisconsin–Madison and an MFA in nonfiction from University of North Carolina Wilmington. She currently lives in her home state's capital where she appreciates badger statuary, studies rhetoric, and teaches writing to undergraduates, high schoolers, and those incarcerated at Oakhill Correctional Institution.

Hannah Smith is a writer living in Dallas, Texas. She received an MFA in poetry from The Ohio State University, where she served as the managing editor of *The Journal*. She is a National Poetry Series finalist, and her poems have been published or are forthcoming in *Gulf Coast*, *Ninth Letter*, *Image*, and elsewhere. Her collaborative chapbook, *Metal House of Cards*, is forthcoming from Finishing Line Press.

Shirley Stephenson's writing has appeared in *Ploughshares*, *Michigan Quarterly Review*, *Fence*, and elsewhere. She works as a nurse practitioner on Chicago's west side. She is pursuing a PhD in the Program for Writers at the University of Illinois Chicago, where she also serves as poet-in-residence at the Institute for Research on Addictions.

Matthew Tuckner received his MFA in creative writing at NYU and is currently a PhD candidate in English/creative writing at University of Utah. His debut collection of poems, *The Decline and Fall of the Roman Empire*, is forthcoming from Four Way Books. His poems have appeared or are forthcoming in *AGNI*, *American Poetry Review*, *The Nation*, *Copper Nickel*, and *Ninth Letter*, among others.

Dāshaun Washington is a poet living in San Francisco and a 2023–2025 Wallace Stegner Fellow in Poetry at Stanford University. His work has received support from Yaddo, the Bread Loaf Writers' Conference, Lighthouse Works, Ucross Foundation, The Watering Hole, and beyond. His poetry has appeared or is forthcoming in *New England Review*, *Poetry*, *The Nation*, *Poem-a-Day*, *American Poetry Review*, and elsewhere.

Alice White is an American poet living in rural France. Originally from Kansas, she holds an MA in English from the University of St. Andrews in Scotland, where she was awarded the King James VI Prize. Her writing has received support from the Hawthornden Foundation, AWP Writer to Writer, the Bread Loaf Writers' Conference, and the Rona Jaffe Foundation. Her poems have appeared or are forthcoming in *Black Warrior Review*, *Gulf Coast*, *The London Magazine*, *New Ohio Review*, *The Poetry Review*, *swamp pink* (formerly *Crazyhorse*), and *The Threepenny Review*.

Jim Whiteside is the author of a chapbook, *Writing Your Name on the Glass* (Bull City Press, 2019), and is a former Wallace Stegner Fellow. He is the recipient of scholarships from the Bread Loaf and Sewanee Writers' conferences, and residencies from the Virginia Center for the Creative Arts and the Cité Internationale des Arts in Paris. His poems have appeared or are forthcoming in *The New York Times*, *The Atlantic*, *The American Poetry Review*, *Poetry*, and *Ploughshares*. Originally from Cookeville, Tennessee, he holds an MFA from the University of North Carolina at Greensboro and lives in Brooklyn, New York.

Originally from Chicago, Lizabeth Yandel is a writer and filmmaker in rural Oregon. She received her MFA in poetry from UC Irvine and was awarded the 2022 University of California Graduate Prize for Excellence in Poetry. Her poems are published or forthcoming in *The Southern Review*, *Copper Nickel*, *Narrative*, *Rattle*, *The American Journal of Poetry*, and took second place in *Palette Poetry*'s 2023 Sappho Prize. She can be found online at lizabethyandel.com

Nicholas Yingling is the author of *The Fire Road* (Barrow Street, 2024). His work has appeared in *Poetry Daily*, *The Adroit Journal*, *32 Poems*, *The Missouri Review*, *Pleiades*, and elsewhere. He received an MA from the University of California, Davis and currently lives in Los Angeles with a one-eared pit bull named Clementine.

Participating Magazines

32 Poems
32poems.com

Able Muse
ablemuse.com

The Account
theaccountmagazine.com

The Adroit Journal
theadroitjournal.org

AGNI
agnionline.bu.edu

Alien Magazine
alienliterarymagazine.com

ALOCASIA
alocasia.org

ANMLY
anmly.org

Apple Valley Review
applevalleyreview.com

ARTS & LETTERS
artsandletters.gcsu.edu

Barrelhouse
barrelhousemag.com

Bayou Magazine
bayoumagazine.org

Beestung
beestungmag.com

Bellevue Literary Review
blreview.org

Beloit Poetry Journal
bpj.org

Bennington Review
benningtonreview.org

Birdfeast
birdfeastmagazine.com

Birmingham Poetry Review
uab.edu/cas/englishpublications/birmingham-poetry-review

Blackbird
blackbird.vcu.edu

Black Warrior Review
bwr.ua.edu

Blood Orange Review
bloodorangereview.com

Bloodroot
bloodrootlit.org

Booth: A Journal
booth.butler.edu

Boulevard
boulevardmagazine.org

Carve Magazine
carvezine.com

Chestnut Review
chestnutreview.com

Cincinnati Review
cincinnatireview.com

Coal Hill Review
coalhillreview.com

Cola Literary Review
colaliteraryreview.com

Copper Nickel
copper-nickel.org

Cutleaf
cutleafjournal.com

december
decembermag.org

Denver Quarterly
du.edu/denverquarterly

DIALOGIST
dialogist.org

The Dodge
thedodgemag.com

Ecotone
ecotonemagazine.org

EVENT Magazine
eventmagazine.ca

Fairy Tale Review
fairytalereview.com

The Fiddlehead
thefiddlehead.ca

Fjords Review
fjordsreview.com

The Florida Review
floridareview.cah.ucf.edu

Foglifter
foglifterjournal.com

Free State Review
freestatereview.com

Fugue
fuguejournal.com

The Georgia Review
thegeorgiareview.com

The Gettysburg Review
gettysburgreview.com

Greensboro Review
greensbororeview.org

Guernica
guernicamag.com

Hayden's Ferry Review
haydensferryreview.com

The Hopkins Review
hopkinsreview.com

After Happy Hour Review
afterhappyhourreview.com

Image
imagejournal.org

Iron Horse
ironhorsereview.com

Jet Fuel Review
jetfuelreview.com

The Journal
english.osu.edu/mfa

The Lascaux Review
lascauxreview.com

Los Angeles Press
thelosangelespress.com

Lucky Jefferson
luckyjefferson.com

The Margins
aaww.org

Michigan Quarterly Review
sites.lsa.umich.edu/mqr

Mid-American Review
casit.bgsu.edu/midamericanreview

Minola Review
minolareview.com

Minyan Magazine
minyanmag.com

Naugatuck River Review
naugatuckriverreview.com

New England Review
nereview.com

Newfound
newfound.org

New Ohio Review
newohioreview.org

New Orleans Review
neworleansreview.org

The Night Heron Barks
nightheronbarks.com

Nimrod International Journal
artsandsciences.utulsa.edu/nimrod/

Nurture
nurtureliterary.com

Okay Donkey
okaydonkeymag.com

Parentheses Journal
parenthesesjournal.com

Passages North
passagesnorth.com

Permafrost
permafrostmag.uaf.edu

Phoebe
phoebejournal.com

Pigeon Pages
pigeonpagesnyc.com

Ploughshares
pshares.org

The Pinch
pinchjournal.com

Poem-A-Day
poets.org/poem-day

Poet Lore
poetlore.com

$ - Poetry Is Currency
poetrycurrency.com

Posit Journal
positjournal.com

Prism Review
sites.laverne.edu/prism-review

Quarterly West
quarterlywest.com

Raleigh Review
RaleighReview.org

Ran Off with the Star Bassoon
ranoffwiththestarbassoon.com

Roanoke Review
roanokereview.org

Room Magazine
roommagazine.com

Salt Hill Journal
salthilljournal.net

Sapiens
sapiens.org

Sewanee Review
thesewaneereview.com

Shenandoah
shenandoahliterary.org

Sho Poetry Journal
shopoetryjournal.com

Sine Theta Magazine
sinetheta.net

Slippery Elm
slipperyelm.findlay.edu

Sonora Review
sonorareview.com

The Southeast Review
southeastreview.org

The Southern Review
thesouthernreview.org

Split Lip Magazine
splitlipthemag.com

Split Rock Review
splitrockreview.org

Sugar House Review
SugarHouseReview.com

Sundog Lit
sundoglit.com

SWWIM Every Day
swwim.org

Tahoma Literary Review
tahomaliteraryreview.com

Terrain
terrain.org

Third Coast
thirdcoastmagazine.com

Thrush Poetry Journal
thrushpoetryjournal.com

Tinderbox Poetry Journal
tinderboxpoetry.com

Up the Staircase Quarterly
upthestaircase.org

Virginia Quarterly Review
vqronline.org

Washington Square Review
washingtonsquarereview.com

Whale Road Review
whaleroadreview.com

wildness
readwildness.com

Willow Springs
willowspringsmagazine.org

ZYZZYVA
zyzzyva.org

Participating Programs

American University Creative Writing Program
american.edu/cas/literature/mfa

Chatham University MFA in Creative Writing
chatham.edu/mfa

City College of New York MFA Program in Creative Writing
ccny.cuny.edu/english/creativewriting

Florida International University MFA in Creative Writing
english.fiu.edu/creative-writing

Hollins University Jackson Center for Creative Writing
hollinsmfa.wordpress.com

Johns Hopkins The Writing Seminars
writingseminars.jhu.edu

Kansas State University MFA in Creative Writing Program
k-state.edu/english/programs/cw

Kent State University Wick Poetry Center
kent.edu/wick

Minnesota State University Mankato Creative Writing Program
english.mnsu.edu/cw

New Mexico State University MFA in Creative Writing
english.nmsu.edu/graduate-programs/mfa

New York University Creative Writing Program
as.nyu.edu/cwp

Northwestern University MA/MFA in Creative Writing
sps.northwestern.edu/program-areas/graduate/creative-writing

The Ohio State University MFA Program in Creative Writing
english.osu.edu/mfa

Ohio University Creative Writing PhD
ohio.edu/cas/english/grad/creative-writing/index.cfm

San Diego State University MFA in Creative Writing
mfa.sdsu.edu

Southeast Missouri State University Master of Arts in English
semo.edu/english

Syracuse University MFA in Creative Writing
english.syr.edu/cw/cw-program.html

Texas Tech University Creative Writing Program
depts.ttu.edu/english/programs_degrees/programs/cw

Texas Tech University Creative Writing Program
depts.ttu.edu/english/cw

UMass Amherst MFA for Poets and Writers
umass.edu/englishmfa

UMass Boston MFA Program in Creative Writing
umb.edu/academics/cla/english/grad/mfa

UNC Greensboro Creative Writing Program
mfagreensboro.org

University of Alabama at Birmingham Graduate Theme in Creative Writing
uab.edu/cas/english/graduate-program/creative-writing

University of Connecticut Creative Writing Program
creativewriting.uconn.edu

University of Idaho MFA in Creative Writing
uidaho.edu/class/english/graduate/mfa-creative-writing

University of Illinois at Chicago Program for Writers
engl.uic.edu/CW

University of Kansas Graduate Creative Writing Program
englishcw.ku.edu

University of Mississippi MFA in Creative Writing
mfaenglish.olemiss.edu

University of Missouri Creative Writing Program
english.missouri.edu/area/creative-writing

University of New Orleans Creative Writing Workshop
uno.edu/writing

University of North Texas Creative Writing
english.unt.edu/creative-writing-0

University of San Francisco MFA in Writing
usfca.edu/mfa

University of Southern Mississippi Center for Writers
usm.edi/writers

University of South Florida MFA in Creative Writing
english.usf.edu/graduate/concentrations/cw/degrees

University of Texas Michener Center for Writers
michener.utexas.edu

University of Utah Creative Writing Program
english.utah.edu

Western Michigan University Creative Writing Program
wmich.edu/english

West Virginia University MFA Program
creativewriting.wvu.edu

The series editor wishes to thank the many poets involved in our first round of reading:

Katilyn Airy, Caroline Erickson, Kate Coleman, ethan evans, mack gregg, Cy March, Lucas Martínez, and MaKshya Tolbert

Special thanks to Jason Coleman and the University of Virginia Press for editorial advice and support,
and to John Barnett of 4 Eyes Design for his cover magic.

Printed in the USA
CPSIA information can be obtained
at www.ICGtesting.com
CBHW042359190524
8768CB00025B/433